Elizabeth Taylor

Twayne's English Authors Series

Kinley E. Roby, Editor

Northeastern University

TEAS 405

ELIZABETH TAYLOR
(1912–1975)
*Photograph reprinted by permission
of A. M. Heath & Co.*

Elizabeth Taylor

By Florence Leclercq

Twayne Publishers • Boston

Elizabeth Taylor

Florence Leclercq

Copyright © 1985 by G. K. Hall & Company
All Rights Reserved
Published by Twayne Publishers
A Division of G. K. Hall & Co.
A publishing subsidiary of ITT
70 Lincoln Street
Boston, Massachusetts 02111

Book Production by Elizabeth Todesco
Book Design by Barbara Anderson

Printed on permanent/durable acid-free
paper and bound in the United States of
America.

Library of Congress Cataloging in Publication Data

Leclercq, Florence, 1950–
  Elizabeth Taylor.

  (Twayne's English authors series; TEAS 405)
  Bibliography: p. 130
  Includes index.
  1. Taylor, Elizabeth, 1912–1975—Criticism and interpretation.
I. Title. II. Series.
PR6039.A928Z75   1985   823'.914   84–25197
ISBN 0–8057–6895–5

PR
6039
A928
-75 *Contents*
1985

About the Author
Preface
Chronology

About the Author

Florence Leclercq was born in Lille, France, in 1950. She graduated from the University of Lille in French and English literature. After receiving her Master's degree in 1972, she began teaching at the University of London and subsequently moved to the University of Ottawa. In 1976, she obtained her doctorate from the University of Lille and took a post at the University of British Columbia. Dr. Leclercq is now engaged in research on the contemporary English novel.

Preface

Elizabeth Taylor published twelve novels and four collections of short stories between 1945 and 1976. Despite the fact that her novels are widely read and that she has constantly received favorable reviews from both critics and fellow novelists, she is comparatively little known. This study examines the reasons for this relative lack of recognition and attempts to reevaluate Taylor's place in the history of the contemporary English novel.

Taylor wrote most of her novels at a time of complete social upheaval which produced an essentially lower-middle-class literature. Yet the mood of the period never made a deep impression on her work. Taylor depicts the gracious upper-middle-class life of middle-aged Thames Valley residents. In an ambient mood of anger and disillusionment she conveys an impression of quiet, well-bred aloofness. Her dispassionate tone may appear disconcerting in the shifting fifties and sixties. Nevertheless, Taylor is aware of the changing social structures even though they do not directly affect her well-protected world. She is not, however, primarily concerned with the difficult adjustment to the postwar world and therefore deals with it with commendable moderation.

Taylor writes novels in the domestic tradition of Jane Austen, whose work reflects neither violence nor ferocity. She is concerned mostly with the simple, ordinary aspects of life. Characterized by sobriety, undertones, and quietness, her novels may strike the reader as deeply British. Taylor constantly underplays violent emotions and escapes into irony instead of loud denunciations. A disciplined craftsman, a champion of the understatement, Taylor will delight those who enjoy the moralist's recourse to social comedy as a means to attaining universal truths. As such, she contrasts favorably with many of her more strident contemporaries and may also reassure those who believe that the undying tradition of Jane Austen is the true course of the English novel.

This study follows Taylor's career from the definite postwar assertion of *At Mrs Lippincote's* to the contemporary statements of *Mrs Palfrey at the Claremont* and *Blaming,* and shows the development of Taylor's social awareness and her progressive acceptance of herself as a contemporary novelist.

I wish to thank the estate of Elizabeth Taylor and Virago Press for permission to quote extracts from Elizabeth Taylor's novels and short stories.

I am also indebted to Professor Kinley Roby for his valuable guidance and encouragements, and to my friend Dr. Elizabeth Davis for her advice and suggestions. Finally, I would like to thank my husband, Dr. Clem Boonekamp, for his cooperation and patience with me while I wrote this book.

Florence Leclercq

Chronology

Chapter One
A Postwar Novelist

At the outset of World War II, when Elizabeth Taylor's first novel was published, the cultural scene was empty and critics felt increasing concern for what they already referred to as "the death of the novel." There was "a growing atmosphere of concern about the literary wasteland, a growing agreement that, somehow, it must be irrigated with new talent."[1]

In 1945, a rebirth of the novel was expected. The intellectual aristocracy of Cambridge, however, had been decimated by the years of war; their few survivors were silent. The break caused by the war proved to be unavoidably irreversible, and the prewar world only left an impression of unreality in everyone's mind. Samuel Hynes notes: "That world [Bloomsbury] died in the war, perhaps symbolically, with the suicide of Mrs. Woolf. It has been succeeded by what seems its opposite—the post-war Welfare-State world, a monster of austerity, uncertainty and mediocrity, of petty anxieties and unrelieved tedium."[2] In the late forties, the British public was in a state of shock. In his book *The Angry Decade,* Kenneth Allsop gives an accurate evaluation of the situation: "Battered by the war and ten years of filthy food, worn-out clothes and austerity, with grime and drabness rubbed into the pores, the British public was in what GPs call a 'run-down condition.' "[3]

The creation of a socialist commonwealth of Great Britain, the leveling of social classes that aimed toward the lowest common denominator, were bound to produce an essentially working-class literature whose main purpose would be to reflect the atmosphere of the period. In 1958, Frank Hilton wrote: "This country is sick, without confidence, neurotic."[4]

The British novel has always strongly reflected the social ambiance of its time. In the sixties, E. M. Forster, who had been silent for years, wrote: "I think one of the reasons why I stopped writing novels is that the social aspect of the world changed so much. I had been accustomed to write about the old-fashioned world with its homes and its family life and its comparative peace. All that went, and though I can think about the new world, I cannot put it into fiction."[5] Forster was, in fact, heralding the emergence of a new generation of writers who were to be the spokesmen of a new class—a class whose prevailing mood was one of anger. In his article "The Un-Angry Young Men," Leslie A. Fiedler describes the emergence of a new generation of writers:

The young British writer has the inestimable advantage of representing a new class on its way into a controlling position in the culture of his country. He is able to define himself against the class he replaces: against the ideal of "Bloomsbury," which is to say, against a blend of homosexual sensibility, upper-class aloofness, liberal politics, and avant-garde literary devices. When he is boorish rather than well-behaved, rudely angry rather than ironically amused, when he is philistine rather than arty—even when he merely writes badly, he can feel he is performing a service for literature, liberating it from the tyranny of a taste based on a world of wealth and leisure which has become quite unreal.[6]

The social climate of the years immediately following the war produced a generation of so-called "angry young men" who lashed out angrily at the shaken structures of the Establishment. The new generation of writers was characterized by deep self-consciousness, extreme class-consciousness, inferiority complexes, and a very obvious—although often misguided—anger. It is in this turmoil of frustration and anger that Elizabeth Taylor took her first steps into the literary world.

Elizabeth Coles, the daughter of Oliver and Elsie Coles, was born in Reading, England, on 3 July 1912. Her mother, whose imagination "lit candles all over the banal scene,"[7] made a deep impression on the child, just as Julia's imagination delighted her son Oliver in *At Mrs. Lippincote's*.

"As a young child," Elizabeth Taylor commented, "I began to write stories and always wanted to be a novelist. . . ."[8] She wrote "plays with three lines in a scene and terrific changes of scenery,"[9] not unlike Sophie Vanbrugh's efforts in *Palladian*. In *A View of the Harbour,* Taylor gently mocks Beth, a writer quite similar to herself, whose reminiscences sound much like the author's:

> "*You* were always lying on your belly on the grass writing 'Volume One' in a new exercise book."
>
> "Writing Volume One is easy," Beth laughed, "I used to start the book wondering what in God's name would come next. . . . The best part of writing a book is when you write the title at the top of the page and your name underneath and then 'Chapter One'! When that's done the best part's over."[10]

Elizabeth Taylor was educated at the Abbey School, Reading, "a school which carries on the name of an eighteenth century school, run by French refugees, at which Mrs. Sherwood, Miss Mitford, and Jane Austen were pupils."[11] In 1930 she left school to become a governess. She later became a librarian at the public library at High Wycombe, an occupation she particularly enjoyed. In 1936 she married John William Kendal Taylor, a manufacturer, and stopped working. Her son, Renny, was born in 1937, her daughter, Joanna, in 1941.

During the war, while her husband, then in the R.A.F, was posted in Scarborough, Elizabeth Taylor wrote the first of her published novels, *At Mrs. Lippincote's.* The book was well received, especially in England. So was her second novel, *Palladian,* published a year later in 1946. With *A View of the Harbour,* which came out in 1947, Elizabeth Taylor started making a name for herself. Encouraged by favorable critics, she began to publish short stories. "A Sad Garden" and "The Light of the Day" appeared in *Harper's* in 1947. A third story, "First Death in Her Life," was later published by the *New Yorker* which, throughout her life, published most of her short stories. These stories were later collected into four volumes: *Hester Lilly and Other Stories* (1954), *The Blush and Other Stories* (1958), *A Dedicated Man and Other Stories* (1965), and *The Devastating Boys and Other Stories* (1972). Most of her novels also received warm appraisals from critics. They include *A Game of Hide and Seek* (1951), *The Sleeping Beauty* (1953), *Angel* (1957), *In a Summer Season* (1961), *The Soul of Kindness* (1964), *The Wedding Group* (1968), *Mrs. Palfrey at the Claremont* (1971), and the posthumous *Blaming* (1976). It is, however, for her short stories that Elizabeth Taylor has gained most recognition throughout the years.

The author has been described as "slight, fair, and grey-eyed, with features that could be oversharp with intelligence if they were not subdued with a considerable understanding for human beings."[12] Speaking about herself, Taylor has made interesting revelations: "I love England and it would be painful to me to consider living in any other place. I find so beautiful, harmonious and evocative, its landscape, style, tradition, even its climate. I should like to feel that the people in my books are essentially English and set down against a truly English background."[13]

The most striking feature about Elizabeth Taylor is indeed how deeply English she is. It is, however, a characteristic she shares with the great majority of the postwar writers, as opposed to writers like Graham Greene or Somerset Maugham. It may also explain why American critics have found it hard to appraise her writing to its full value, just as they have had difficulty with other present-day novelists such as Kingsley Amis, Alan Sillitoe, or John Wain. William Cooper, in his *Scenes from Life,* evokes, with mock indignation, a young writer turned down by American publishers for being "too British": "Too British . . . how could it be too British when I *was* British, when all my forbears, as far back as any records went, had been British?"[14]

Elizabeth Taylor's British characteristics may amount to insularity. She very rarely sets her novels or short stories abroad, and only does so with a certain reluctance. She is not, however, British in the same way as her fellow novelists are. Whereas they describe drab conditions of life in Yorkshire, or the Midlands, Elizabeth Taylor sets most of her novels in the Thames Valley, from the Cotswolds to the Thames estuary, an attractive—and very selective—part of England, the region she comes from and knows best. Some of her novels or short stories are also set in London, once again in select areas such as St. John's Wood, Hampstead, or Chelsea.

Even though Taylor writes that "The background is part of the characters,"[15] it is clear that the background is not essential to the characters who come to her first. Taylor concentrates on people, then tries to imagine their lives. If her characters are the product of their background, whether physical, psychological, or social, this fact seems to bear little significance to her as a novelist. Unlike novels by her contemporaries, Taylor's books do not have much of a sociological impact.

It is the essence of Elizabeth Taylor's work that she deals with the rare privileged classes who have not been as affected by the war as the working or lower-middle classes. Material contingencies are mentioned delicately, tactfully, lightly, as though insisting upon them would be slightly improper. The "shilling for the meter," the strict rationing of cigarettes, "beer rather than spirits" are notions quite foreign to her fictional world. Taylor cannot be described as a realistic writer even though her occasional attempts at realism succeed. Her vision of the world is the vision of the artists who figure prominently in her books. In *A Wreath of Roses,* Frances, for whom Taylor shows considerable affection, sees life "with tenderness and intimacy. With sentimentality too. . . ." Elizabeth Taylor uses Frances to epitomize her own vision of the world, her own conception of life: "An English sadness like a veil over all I painted, until it became ladylike and nostalgic, governessy, utterly lacking in ferocity, brutality, violence."[16] It is precisely that ferocity, that brutality, that violence, which Taylor perceives in the world and yet refuses to translate into fiction.

If Taylor does not reflect the mood of the period, the pervading anger, if her work cannot be read as a period piece, since she deals with too rare and privileged a class, then what does she do? Where does she fit in? Kingsley Amis, one of her fervent admirers, has brought up that very question:

Those readers who have enjoyed and admired the work of Mrs. Elizabeth Taylor ever since *At Mrs. Lippincote's* was published in 1945, may well ask themselves why it is that so gifted a writer has yet to find the recognition she deserves. It is true that by now she is all laurelled o'er with recommendations and choices and laudatory quotes, mainly from older reviewers, and she must have a considerable following among those whose opinions do not get into print. But in surveys of the modern novel, whether printed or oral, she never seems to find a place. Why not? Such a deprivation may seem readily endurable, but how has it arisen?[17]

One of the reasons for this lack of recognition may well be that Elizabeth Taylor deals with a microcosm, a small section of English life. She usually describes a limited number of characters isolated from the outside world, then studies their interactions on each other. She very rarely offers descriptions of a wide variety of people, nor does she delve into the social classes about which she knows little. Her fictional world is confined to artists, writers, well-to-do businessmen, wealthy idle women, picturesque old ladies, with the occasional shop girl, local gossip, eccentric cook, grumpy charwoman, and, here and there, a few disgruntled or baffled young people. Her protagonists are a very respectable assortment of people. Whatever the intensity of the conflicts that tear them apart, whatever turmoil of emotions they experience, the surface of their lives remains smooth and unrippled. At the age of twelve, Taylor had a poem rejected for being "nice but a trifle stormy,"[18] which made her resolve never to be stormy again. The atmosphere of her novels is dramatically peaceful, which sets her poles apart from Iris Murdoch, Storm Jameson, or Elizabeth Jane Howard. In her writing, Taylor displays a remarkable control of emotions, a mastery of the understatement. Her tone is that of a quiet, well-bred English lady.

When discussing "contemporary" women novelists such as Rebecca West and Rosamond Lehmann, Anthony Burgess notes that they "have for the most part resisted the urge to be 'contemporary' . . . as though they were unsure of their audiences or found difficulty in making contact with the post-war world."[19] Elizabeth Taylor has met with the same difficulty; her contacts with the postwar world remain flimsy, unreal. Her ambivalence lies in the fact that, on the one hand, she fights to reconcile herself with the reality of postwar England, to have her place among contemporary novelists, and on the other hand, she has by-passed the difficulty by establishing her position in a lasting tradition of the English novel.

When Burgess defines the "Austen touch" as "humour, delicacy, restraint, common sense, a limited social field," he also gives a satisfactory account of Taylor's characteristics as a writer. Not unlike Elizabeth Bowen to whom she is often compared—even though Bowen is an "older" writer—Taylor finds difficulty adjusting to the drab conditions of welfare-state Britain and permeates her work with nostalgia. Taylor's tone is also comparable to Bowen's, their social fields equally limited. Above all, they belong to the same literary current, the same "outmoded" yet undying tradition set by Jane Austen's "novels of sensibility."

The tradition of Jane Austen does not represent the current trend of the English novel, however. The years following the war have witnessed the revival of realism which has given the English novel a much-needed new lease of life. In *The Novelist at the Crossroads,* David Lodge writes:

The situation of the novelist today may be compared to a man standing at a crossroads. The road on which he stands (I am thinking primarily of the English novelist) is the realistic novel, the compromise between fictional and empirical modes. In the 'fifties there was a strong feeling that this was the main road, the central tradition, of the English novel, coming down through the Victorians and Edwardians, temporarily diverted by modernist experimentalism, but subsequently restored (by Orwell, Isherwood, Greene, Waugh, Powell, Angus Wilson, C. P. Snow, Amis, Sillitoe, Wain, etc., etc.) to its true course.[20]

Kingsley Amis is more specific than Lodge. He sees, in the rebirth of realism, a revival of interest for Fielding in particular. In his article "Laughter's to be Taken Seriously," Amis writes: "John Wain and Iris Murdoch, for instance, are two young writers who, though far too often compared and in most ways poles apart, are alike in their evident feeling that the novel of a consistent tone, moving through a recognized and restricted cycle of emotional keys, was out-moded. Without having to picture such writers going through an eureka-routine with a copy of 'Tom Jones,' one can still detect in them some kind of affinity with its author." Not only does Amis himself belong to the writers thus described, so do Burgess, Cooper, Sillitoe, Braine, Enright, and many others. Amis then adds: "Their attempt has been to combine the violent and the absurd, the grotesque and the romantic, the farcical and the horrific within a single novel."[21] Amis accurately describes the necessary ingredients that make up the contemporary novel: the mixture of anger and irony treated in a strong realistic manner.

Elizabeth Taylor, whose novels of a consistent tone move through "a recognized and restricted cycle of emotional keys," is not outmoded, however. She is uncontemporary. She is in the Austen line—a fact that can hardly be denied—and this tradition of the English novel is not likely to die. Yet, she is regarded as an outsider. Her lack of anger, her failure to denounce the class structure, her sympathy for the world she lives in, her gentleness, her quiet tone have, strangely enough, excluded her from the main drift of the contemporary English novel.

As an outsider, she has received high critical acclaim, especially from fellow novelists. When *At Mrs. Lippincote's* was published in 1945, L. P. Hartley wrote, "It is a book for the epicure, who will delight in its deftness, its compression, its under- and over-tones, no less than for the general reader, who will find satisfaction and a certain solace in its rather sad philosophy."[22] Elizabeth Bowen found that there was "an exciting distinction about every page she [wrote]."[23] Rosamond Lehmann described her as "sophisticated, sensitive, and brilliantly amusing, with a kind of stripped, piercing feminine wit and a power of creating and maintaining a fine nervous tension."[24] Brigid Brophy wrote, "Mrs. Taylor has always been an excellently unpretentious writer: if she had a fault it used to be that she was (artistically) under-ambitious."[25] Kingley Amis called her "one of the liveliest and most forceful of our younger novelists."[26]

Elizabeth Taylor has been called "the poor man's Virginia Woolf." She is clearly indebted to Virginia Woolf whom she greatly admires. Taylor has never disguised her preference for books in which practically nothing happened. Any resemblance, however, is one of spirit and does not do her true justice. According to Arthur Mizener who coined the phrase, it would be more accurate to call Taylor "the modern man's Jane Austen."[27] The qualifications used to justify such an appelation include "feminine," "perceptive," "middle class," "domestic," "English," and "ironic," and all of them are equally true. Taylor, however, has developed her own individuality, namely, through her careful, meticulous craftsmanship. Gerald Sykes succinctly summarized her personal contribution to the contemporary novel when he wrote in 1954: "At all times Mrs. Taylor conveys a profoundly healthy tenderness with a consummate economy of style. She has a woman's unfooled realism and sympathy, and uses them to give quiet enjoyment to all who believe, despite our estranging new conveniences, that man is still the best show of all."[28]

It is Elizabeth Taylor's personal contribution to the postwar novel that this study aims at establishing. Although she belongs to an older tradition in spirit and tone, although—at times—

she fights against the current trend toward realism, she still struggles to have her place among contemporary novelists and displays an eminently mature and consummate literary technique.

Chapter Two

The Paradox of the
First Two Novels

At Mrs. Lippincote's was published in 1945, *Palladian* in 1946.
Both novels were well received. Critics praised Elizabeth Taylor's sensitivity, subtlety, and deftness. The two books, however,
have very little in common. While *Palladian* has been described
as written in "the English manor-house convention,"[1] *At Mrs.
Lippincote's* shows a definite sense of innovation. While *Palladian*
is permeated with an obvious prewar mood, *At Mrs. Lippincote's*
appears as a definite postwar statement.

Written in 1945, a critical time for the English novel, *At
Mrs. Lippincote's* is one of the first significant utterances of the
postwar novel. In fact, Elizabeth Taylor's first novel somehow
conveys the impression that her contribution to the English novel
might be largely sociological. *At Mrs. Lippincote's* reflects, with
fair accuracy, the social atmosphere of the end of the war. However, the feeling that Taylor's novels might have a sociological
impact was soon dispelled through the publication of *Palladian,*
her second novel. The two novels contrast strikingly. While
At Mrs. Lippincote's appears as an attempt to come to terms with
the grim reality of wartime England, *Palladian* seems a prudent
retreat into the past and an attempt to escape political and social
pressures.

At Mrs. Lippincote's

At Mrs. Lippincote's is a disturbing first novel that displays a
strong individuality from the writer. Although the book is clearly
marked by the war and postwar period, it manages at the same
time to be ahead of its time in tone. The story, largely autobiographical, is very simple. Julia Davenant, the wife of an R.A.F.
officer, follows her husband to northern England during the

war. The novel deals with her difficulties in settling down, her deteriorating relationship with her husband Roddy, her problems with Roddy's cousin Eleanor, who lives with them, and her closeness to her son Oliver. Taylor offers a lively description of the daily life of an independent young woman who goes through an identity crisis and who finally manages to come to terms with the stark reality of her life.

Elizabeth Taylor's first novel succeeds mostly out of the force with which she creates a unique central character. Julia Davenant is an exciting literary figure, created barely a decade before other protagonists such as Joe Lunn, Charles Lumley, Jim Dixon, Joe Lampton, etc.[2] Like them, she is in constant conflict with her surroundings. As she is also implicitly described as a feminist, the daughter of a suffragette, she can easily be labeled as an "angry young woman." The attribute is paradoxical, however, for "angry young men" only reject, as a reaction, what they feel rejected by. Similarly, Julia cannot conform because she suffers from a social inferiority complex. Her attitudes, however, are extremely refreshing. Her refusal to accept anything at its face value endears her immediately to the reader: "Julia had a strange gift of coming to a situation freshly, peculiarly untarnished by preconceived ideas, whether of her own preconception or the world's."[3] She feels the need to challenge generally accepted concepts or conventions. Yet her attitudes do not always ring true. For example, while Julia resents her status as a wife, the reader may detect a touch of complacency in her behavior and social attitudes. Paradox and conflict are the mark of her personality, a fact of which she is aware. She realizes the irony of her situation, the impropriety of biting the hand that feeds her: "I am a parasite, I follow my man round like a piece of luggage or part of a travelling harem. He is under contract to provide for me, but where he does so is for him to decide" (199). The complacent touch is not always present. On one occasion, Julia loses her temper: "I'm not hanging about like a woman in a book for my husband to come home drunk. There's only one answer to that, and that's a conventional one, a vulgar one, the rolling-pin one, and I can't do it" (129).

Although Julia's lucidity and clear-mindedness set her apart from the "angry young men" class, she shares with them the same ambiguous and paradoxical social attitudes. Like them, she behaves like a social iconoclast at times, deliberately ignoring class distinctions and ranks. When she treats the commanding officer with the same familiarity as a corporal, she creates scenes of sheer comedy which Taylor revels in depicting. Yet Julia also wishes to be socially accepted, to be part of what she dimly recognizes as the Establishment. She does not feel at ease in Mrs. Lippincote's house. The picture of Mrs. Lippincote's wedding group on the wall strikes her as a permanent reminder of her own failure to conform. Mrs. Lippincote's visit, toward the end of the book, appears as the final judgment and ensuing condemnation. Taylor excels at describing ironically her heroine's lack of social graces.

> She crossed the hall at a casual pace, and with a look of hostility, which she imagined was an air of self possession, opened the door.
> "I am Mrs. Lippincote."
> Superfluous statement. . . .
> "How do you do." Julia held back the door and stretched her lips in welcome. Accompanying Mrs. Lippincote across her own hall, she heard (but could discover no means of stopping) her own insincerities, one after another: pleasure at meeting, gratitude for benefits conferred, humility at living in Mrs. Lippincote's house. Recklessly she admired and condoled, apologised for the war and felt able to promise better things for the future. (161)

Elizabeth Taylor's ironic description of a character plagued by painful self-consciousness parallels the portrait of another protagonist, Jim Dixon, created by Kingsley Amis. Like Jim, Julia watches herself with horrified eyes. The paradox of Julia's social attitudes lies in the fact that, while she feels unable at times to grasp social rules and behave with decorum, while she fails to conform yet wishes to do so, she also never fails to pass judgment on her fellow beings. She, therefore, displays a somewhat crude class-consciousness. On one occasion, she happens to drink brandy with someone whom she considers her social inferior: " 'Here I am sitting in a summer house with the dregs of society,' Julia thought placidly, wondering what Roddy was doing at the moment" (133). She judges her companion and finds him socially wanting. Such an attitude leads the reader to believe that Julia's ignorance of class distinctions and her rejection of conventions spring largely from affectation.

This contradiction in her character is similar to Jim Dixon's. Yet although Taylor can be as amusing as Amis, she does not insist on the comic aspect of her central character as Amis does. Julia's uneasiness never causes her to behave in a totally uncontrollable manner.

Julia's feminism is also ambivalent in the sense that there is no fighting spirit in her. However sound her views may be, clearly reflecting the author's, she never asserts them in a convincing manner. In her discussion about girls' education, namely, about the value of learning Greek, Julia displays much common sense. To the question, "What use will it be to her when she leaves school? Will it cook her husband's dinner?" she replies:

"No, it won't do that, but it will help her to endure doing it, perhaps. If she is to cook while she is at school, then there will be that thing less for her to learn when she's grown up; but, if she isn't to learn Greek at school, then she will never learn it afterwards. And learning Greek at school is like storing honey against the winter."

"But what use is it?" he persisted.

"Men can be educated; women must be trained," she said sorrowfully. (107)

Clearly, Julia gives in just a little too easily. Taylor does not seem bent upon using her as a vehicle for her own ideas. *At Mrs. Lippincote's* cannot be considered as a feminist manifesto. Julia's opinions are sometimes even viewed in a hilarious manner. When she is told that Roddy will not be back for dinner, Eleanor suggests:

"We can manage with some cheese."

"Why? Why? How did this notion get round that women cook only for men? Why, indeed, should we manage with some cheese, just because our—our sexual organs are different?" Julia stormed.

Eleanor sat down at the bottom step and giggled weakly. . . .

" 'Sexual organs' sounded grand," Eleanor wept, "you are getting to be quite a lady."

Julia went happily to the kitchen. They managed with some cheese. (58)

Elizabeth Taylor makes it clear, at times, that she does not fully endorse Julia's attitudes or conceptions. She, in effect, warns

the reader, early in the novel, to take Julia with a grain of
salt: "Could she have taken for granted a few of those generalisa-
tions invented by men and largely acquiesced in by women
(that women live by their hearts, men by their heads, that love
is woman's whole existence, and especially that sons should respect their fathers), she would have eased her own life and
other people's" (26). There is, once again, a certain ambivalence
in Taylor's treatment of Julia whose views she seems to advocate
at times, and to criticize at other times.

At Mrs. Lippincote's strongly reflects the uneasiness of the mid-
forties. A strong mood of nostalgia pervades the novel, as it
will all of Taylor's stories. The title of the novel is significant.
Mrs. Lippincote only appears once in the novel, yet her presence
is continuously felt by Julia and the other characters. Mrs. Lippincote represents the old world in the process of crumbling, a
class that has died and whose surviving members often appear
as ghosts from the past. Julia frequently looks at the picture
of Mrs. Lippincote's wedding group with nostalgia: " 'And now
it's all finished,' Julia thought. 'They had that lovely day and
the soup tureen and meat dishes, servants with frills and stream-
ers, children. They set out that day as if they were laying the
foundations of something' " (10). Julia clearly refers to the years
immediately preceding World War I, a period that retro-
spectively appears as an era of innocence and happiness.

The importance of Mrs. Lippincote's wedding group is notice-
able throughout the novel. At times of crisis, Julia frequently
looks up and stares at the faded picture: "She looked at Mrs.
Lippincote on her wedding day as she was often to look at
her in the future. Nothing of her security, in these days. What
would she have said to this? No home of one's own, no servant,
no soup tureen, no solid phalanx of sisters, or sisters-in-law,
to uphold her. . . ." (12). What Julia is lamenting is the disintegration of the world around her, the upheaval brought about
by the war. She senses a complete change in the social structures
and feels lost in an alien world she does not understand. Taylor's
first novel introduces what will be a central theme in her work:
the theme of transition between two worlds. In *At Mrs. Lippincote's,* Taylor describes the end of an epoch and expresses,
through Julia, her fear for the future.

At Mrs. Lippincote's contains numerous references to the

Brontës. One of the characters refers to *The Tenant of Wildfell Hall* as "a fairly haunting study of disintegration, *n'est-ce pas?*" (176). These apparently careless words reflect a constant feature of the novel. As in the novels of the Brontës, *At Mrs. Lippincote's* displays a particular concern with the concept of disintegration. There is a distinct analogy between the destruction of the outside world and the disintegration of the subtle web of human relationships. Taylor draws a careful parallel between the crumbling of the Old World's structures, brought about by the war, and the snapping of family ties. In her first novel, Taylor already shows her overwhelming preoccupation with human relationships, with the failure to "connect," and with the ensuing loneliness that her characters bitterly experience.

To stress the irreconcilable difference between human beings, Elizabeth Taylor resorts implicitly to Virginia Woolf's distinction between the two drastically different types of men: "On the one hand, the steady goers of superhuman strength . . . on the other, the gifted, the inspired. . . ."[4] Julia and her son Oliver belong the latter group, Roddy and his cousin Eleanor, to the former. The gap between them cannot be bridged. Consequently, the relationship between husband and wife which, at the best of times, has never been good, quickly deteriorates throughout the novel when circumstances put pressures on them. Roddy and Julia see eye to eye and discover they are complete strangers. Roddy, in particular, sees Julia as a child who will never grow up: "When he had married Julia, he had thought her woefully ignorant of the world; had looked forward, indeed, to assisting in her development. But she had been grown up all the time; or, at least, she had not changed. The root of the trouble was not ignorance at all, but the refusal to accept" (105). On the other hand, Roddy and Eleanor are two of a kind. Not only do they understand each other perfectly, but they feel they also understand Julia. Their conversation, one day when Julia has been staying out late, is quite revealing of their thinking alike, and Taylor emphasizes the communion of thoughts between the two cousins. " 'She gets such strange notions,' they said, 'and impulses.' 'I am a little worried about Julia lately,' said Eleanor. 'She is moody and unlike herself.' Roddy suppressed the thought that Julia had been unlike herself ever since he had first known her" (136).

To exemplify the difficulty of the relationship between two so totally different persons as Julia and Roddy, Taylor uses the image of a mirror, a recurring motif in her fiction. People, she implies, distort each other according to their subconscious wishes or through projections of their own selves. In the mirror, Julia watches her husband dispassionately, seeing him as the worldly stranger he really is.

She said: "I went to see Mr. Taylor, but he was dead."
He was looking at himself in the mirror. He had a brush in his hand. His rosy face crumpled like a baby's.
"Oh, dear, all the stages we must now go through," she thought with cynical detachment. "We haven't even begun yet—incredulity, dismay, terror, anger, indignation, self-pity. Perhaps curiosity and sarcasm wedged in also." The sight of his face in the mirror only convinced her of what she knew already, that in all her crises his help would be denied her, because he could not become Julia, he could only be himself. (187–88)

Neither Roddy nor Julia can cope with each other's emotions. Roddy's sole concerns are conventions, respectability and success. He is presented as a staunch supporter of Darwin's theory of survival and shows contempt for the poor, the weak, and the unsuccessful.

In a sense, Taylor uses the mirror characters to emphasize the possibility, however improbable, of genuine relationships. From the start of the novel, the author stresses the incompleteness of Julia's life and the young woman's desperate need for understanding. Julia senses and fears her own disintegration. When she prepares to go out, she cannot help feeling revealing anticipation: "What it was she hoped for she had not asked herself, yet she did realise dimly that only among other people might she find what she sought, some other person whose words would link together with hers, with whom, she now thought, leaning forward to colour her lips imperfectly, some chord might be struck" (72). The character who can be seen as a part of Julia's psyche, Julia's counterpart in the novel, is Mallory, Roddy's superior and a man who, behind a rough exterior, hides a great sensitivity. To Roddy's dismay, Julia and Mallory become great friends, in spite of Julia's total disregard for conventions and her lack of respect for the senior officer. The account of their first meeting exemplifies Taylor's ironic approach.

From the hall, she could see the violet and yellow shape of him through the glass door. Having seen him mopping himself a moment before, she could forgive him easily the manner of dark silence in which he entered the house.

"Well?" he began at once, "aren't you going to offer me tea?"

The answer to that is a dipping curtsey and a graceful gesture with the bell rope. Who would respond? she wondered and looked up at him and smiled. He thought it was a strange smile and said so, in a raised voice, trying to remember if she were deaf, seeing in her expression the willingness to hear of those who cannot. . . .

She lifted her face and gave him one of her rare smiles, quite different from the other. "If you had a long cloak" (her hands described it for him) "and whiskers," (she laughed) "then you'd be Rochester to the life. And Oliver would think so, too. Are you trying to be he?" (He is too old, though, she thought.) (48)

It is not too early in their relationship for the reader to see that a chord has been struck between them. Sensing Julia's intense loneliness, Mallory tries to hold out a hand in the darkness where she confines herself: " 'Don't turn to shadow because I draw near to you,' he implored" (111). Yet the relationship ends in failure. What Mallory hoped to achieve—to secure Julia's marriage—fails miserably. They part with little hope of ever meeting again. The fact that even friendships are doomed is a manifestation of Taylor's basic pessimism.

Another minor character plays an important part in the novel because he embodies the author's relentless concern for loneliness. Mr. Taylor personifies loneliness, a fact that draws Julia and him together more securely than happiness could. Their first meeting, after a long period of time, occurs at a dramatic moment in Julia's life: " 'I am quite alone,' she thought. 'In that house there are Roddy and Eleanor ranged against me, facing me from a great distance, like cliffs one sees from a long way off, with no birds flying or flags waving, or windows glinting, not a sign of recognition at all.' She got on a bus headed for the prison." (93–94). Once the owner of a popular French restaurant in Soho, Mr. Taylor was bombed out and forced to seek refuge in northern England where he meets Julia who used to be one of his favorite patrons. Mr. Taylor, a pathetic figure, mourns his past life, his destroyed restaurant which symbolized, in his mind, his former respectability. On a deeper level, Elizabeth Taylor uses this character to express the essential longing for the prewar years, a period of bygone innocence. It is not yet felt that this period is never to return, but Mr. Taylor manages to convey the author's feeling of impending gloom. Julia and Mr. Taylor share the same resigned perceptions of life. A very sick man with nothing to live for, Mr. Taylor is ready to give up the fight. Now the part-owner of a third-rate nightclub, bossed by a woman whom he calls his secretary, the man completely collapses in front of Julia's horrified eyes. Their last meeting before his death, although undoubtedly melodramatic, still retains a pathetic and poignant quality. When offered genuine sympathy, Mr. Taylor breaks down: "At this, covering his face with one hand only, he vomited up a few sobs, a tear or two fell through his fingers. Even in the gathering darkness she could see that, his wet fingers, and a tear running down inside his wrist into his sleeve. With a sensation of utter revulsion, she put her arm across his back and with awkward caresses, like a child, tried to comfort him" (135).

The author stresses the childish aspects of Julia's personality in an attempt to prove that Julia will escape destruction through this special grace of hers. In Taylor's fiction, children are presented as privileged beings. The closeness of the relationship between Oliver and his mother helps her to overcome her loneliness, while the little boy is fascinated by his bookish mother. The description Taylor offers of Oliver is extremely evocative. She presents him as a little bookworm who lives in a literary world where fictional characters have more reality than real people. Oliver's love for books—a trait that Taylor clearly finds endearing, for her portraits of children in general, and of Oliver in particular, are always infused with considerable sympathy—manifests itself by his obvious way of regarding them not as mere objects, but as endowed with a life of their own. Oliver cannot bear to have a scary book in his room at night and will usually leave it on his doormat or windowsill.

Yet in her picture of children, Elizabeth Taylor sometimes errs. However convincing Oliver and his little friend, Felicity, may be, their ways of expressing themselves are occasionally at odds. They are made to sound at times like sophisticated grown-ups, at times like three-year-old infants. In short, Taylor does not always show much of an ear for dialogue. Her strong point in characterization lies in her ironical treatment of her characters. Her real forte is best displayed in the treatment of yet another character.

In Eleanor, the forty-year-old self-deluding spinster, Taylor has excelled herself to the point of cruelty. Her introduction to Eleanor, whom she presents as the example of a wasted existence, is bitingly sarcastic: "She was forty and unmarried, she had a little money in Imperial Tobacco, a royal-blue evening dress, and was in love with her cousin, for whom, as they say, she would have laid down her life with every satisfaction" (14). Taylor also delights in describing Eleanor's peculiar relationship with Chris Aldridge, the communist carpentry master at the school where she teaches. Eleanor thrives on tragedy and sees herself as a tragic figure in a tale of her own making. She confides to Aldridge that she had a breakdown. " 'You must have had some shock?' She hesitated. 'Yes. Look, the lilac trees are in bud!' she cried with bright artificiality. She tried to resist the temptation, struggled and failed. 'My—a dear friend was reported missing, then killed, then, after a long time, a prisoner of war' " (45). Taylor pitilessly mocks the relationship between the two pathetic characters who seem both given to role-playing. Aldridge also confides in Eleanor. " 'It is really not interesting to anyone but myself,' he said, with steady modesty, 'but a shock to me, naturally. The doctor has told me I have three months to live.' 'Three months!' cried Eleanor, as if she could have comprehended four, or six, but not three" (54). Even Julia is used by the author to bring out the irony of the relationship. She indulges in derisive remarks: " 'His time must be nearly up, surely,' said Julia. 'It is going to be embarrassing for us all if he is going to over-run it' " (151). Mr. Aldridge, however, shows no sign of dying. Apart from providing scenes of comedy, he is instrumental in introducing Eleanor to his friends from the Party.

Though Taylor mocks Eleanor mercilessly throughout the novel, the characterization of the cousin supports the central themes of disintegration and loneliness. Like Julia, Eleanor longs to be accepted and to be needed. Eleanor's loneliness consequently manifests itself in her sudden interest for communism. Although she is dimly aware that her newly found friends do not need her, that their friendliness is not quite sincere—for Taylor makes it clear that there is hypocrisy in all circles—Eleanor deludes herself that the situation will soon change.

The end of the novel is particularly grim, bringing about the complete disintegration of the household. Julia faces the fact that her marriage to Roddy is nothing more than a social convention. Eleanor leaves them to go her own way. In the middle of the general confusion, Mrs. Lippincote quietly moves back into her dilapidated house.

It could appear that *At Mrs. Lippincote's* is a pessimistic novel written by a cynical young woman with little faith in human nature. It is undeniable that the relationships described are shown as ephemeral or bound to disintegrate. However, the novel's final note is not sour. Julia and her son Oliver come out of the final chaos alive and, curiously enough, unchanged, if not undisturbed. However somber the descriptions of the disintegrating world may be, there is, in *At Mrs. Lippincote's,* a saving grace: the impression conveyed by the author of her heroine's immunity. While Jim Dixon is saved by luck, Julia Davenant is rescued by her basic self-reliance. In the dispiriting conditions of postwar England, this new protagonist's extremely refreshing outlook, that of a child, gives the novel its originality and its brilliance.

Palladian

While *At Mrs. Lippincote's* shows some form of innovation in the individuality of its central character and in the deft irony of the writing, *Palladian* appears as a definite setback. The two novels contrast sharply in tone and genre, yet they are united by several factors. First, they are both autobiographical. *At Mrs. Lippincote's* is based on Elizabeth Taylor's life in Yorkshire during the war. *Palladian* alludes to the author's experience as a governess before her marriage. Second, the two novels are equally under the auspices of the Brontë sisters. While *At Mrs. Lippincote's* contains many references to the life of the three sisters, *Palladian* seems to be an attempt at the genre of novels they wrote.

It is indeed difficult to decide what Elizabeth Taylor attempted to do when she wrote *Palladian*. The basic situation is that of a poor young girl, plain and obscure, who, upon leaving school, finds she has to work as a governess, subsequently falls in love with her employer, and marries him. This unoriginal plot is slightly reminiscent of *Jane Eyre*, a point the author seems intent upon making.

At the first meeting between the young governess Cassandra Dashwood and her employer Marion Vanbrugh, the intentions of the author are made quite clear: " 'How are you going to get on with Sophy?' he asked. 'I hope—I think—I shall do my—' she began to falter, in a little governessy voice. She knew that Jane Eyre had answered up better than that to her Mr. Rochester"[5]. The young heroine seems forcibly cast into the role of a modern Jane Eyre and the reader cannot help detecting, at times, a touch of authorial constraint in the various typecast characters. They also fail to convince. Cassandra is a very pallid Jane Eyre, indeed: young, inexperienced, constantly frightened, with a complete lack of the independence of spirit that characterized Charlotte Brontë's heroine. Marion Vanbrugh, frail and neuralgia-ridden, strikes the reader as an ironical antithesis of Rochester. He conforms more adequately to the author's idea of Edgar Linton's personality. There are, in fact, elements of *Wuthering Heights* in *Palladian*. Under the same roof as Marion who mourns his beautiful and frivolous wife, Violet, lives Tom, his cousin and the disconsolate lover of the long-dead woman. Once again, Elizabeth Taylor acknowledges her sources. Tom cannot forgive Violet for marrying Marion: "*She* did it. She turned me into a sort of glowering Heathcliff. But she *was* punished. A great deal. More than she deserved" (208).

The situation strikes a note of unreality in the middle of the twentieth century. The whole setting, in fact, is unreal, as unreal as the old Palladian house, a mere facade behind which lies a world of idle young men, nannies, and governesses. The fact that the house is crumbling and its inhabitants appear degenerated—a slight attempt at realism—does little to reassure the reader. The house is also completely cut off from the outside world. The only encroachment of reality upon that fantasy world lies in the presence of a nearby pub. The wife of the publican, the buxom Mrs. Veal, is lost in speculations about the nearby house: "She could never imagine life up at the 'big house,' as she called it to herself, could have pictured grandeur but could find no standard for the lives they led, met as she so continually was by hints of dilapidation, of servants giving orders to employers, of discomforts and shabbiness, which she herself could not have endured" (181).

A major flaw in Taylor's creation of setting is her heavy, almost ironical reliance on clichés. At the first meeting between Cassandra and Marion, she makes Cassandra say: " 'He will do to fall in love with,' Cassandra thought with some relief" (46). This specific remark produces an embarrassing effect upon the reader. The recurrence of similar clichés almost suggests satire at times. Yet there is an intentness of purpose which seems at odds with any possibility of satire. One may conclude that Elizabeth Taylor attempted a genuine adaptation of Charlotte Brontë's theme but failed to strike the note of reality that would have ensured credibility.

For the first and only time, Taylor's achievement in characterization fails to convince. Her protagonists have been accurately described as "peering out at you through a veil."[6] They are flimsy, blurred, hastily sketched. Tinty, the equivalent in the story of Mrs. Fairfax in *Jane Eyre,* is succinctly described as "a spiderish lady." Tom, the drinker, is a little too predictable: " 'I am drinking myself to death,' said Tom. It was melodramatic, but, like all melodrama, had the seeds of great tragedy in it. 'I am wasted. No use. I am done for' " (80). His relationship with the obliging Mrs. Veal from the village pub, whom he uses and despises, runs along conventional patterns. Her meekness provokes his cruelty: "She smiled gallantly, controlling her trembling lips. It was the worst thing she could have done. Tom could not bear stoicism in those he hurt, could not bear the guilt of forcing them into such courage" (182–83).

The creation of Cassandra, the central character, does not carry conviction. Taylor even writes: "Cassandra, sitting there with the broken flint walls arching above her, felt that she was unreal" (99). The young girl is constantly made to behave like a stereotyped governess and her whole behavior follows a set of clichés. When she ponders her relationship with Marion, she realizes that "Before she saw him or spoke to him, she had determined to love him, as if she were a governess in a book" (228). Cassandra also feels the need to conform to her idea of a modern Jane Eyre, and this determination results in several ludicrous passages. Once, as she watches someone eat, "Cassandra's mouth watered, although on account of her love sickness, the worm i' the bud, she would have refused food in Marion's presence" (124). The whole relationship between the two protagonists seems to follow the pattern of lesser romances. Dialogues can be particularly awkward: " 'Apart from Sophy, do you want to go away?' In her agitation her heart cried: 'I love you.' Aloud in a prim voice, she said: 'No. You asked me about Sophy. And that was what I told you' " (100).

The denouement is according to the best tradition of romances. The unlikeliness of the ending is bound to disappoint Taylor's readers. Tom and Mrs. Veal exchange revealing comments: " 'He has gone after the governess and I think he will ask her to marry him.' 'What if she refuses?' Mrs. Veal asked, not able to believe in Marion's success. 'She won't. It is never done' " (212). The ending is, as Taylor sees it, a happy ending. Yet, she fails to be convincing although, until the last paragraph, she appears to be trying. The neuralgia-ridden Marion in his big dilapidated house seems an unlikely husband for the schoolgirlish Cassandra. Rayner Heppenstal writes: "In the end, Miss Taylor does not reassure. Unpleasant consequences are likely to ensue upon this marriage."[7] Taylor ends the novel on an ambiguous note, as if she wanted to free herself from the consequences of her story: "When Marion and Cassandra went indoors, only a lopsided hen was left to enliven the facade, for Nanny and Mrs. Adams had withdrawn their heads. The hen pecked between the cracks of the terrace paving stones and wandered into the hall. But as the dark shadows of indoors fell coldly across it like a knife, it turned and tottered back into the sunshine" (240).

Besides its reliance on stereotypes and clichés, Taylor's second novel is characterized by a new melodramatic trend. One of the characters exclaims: "We shall have had our fill of gossip and melodrama" (209). Not only is *Palladian* linked, in the author's mind, to *Jane Eyre* and *Wuthering Heights,* but it also bears some resemblance to Daphné du Maurier's *Rebecca.* The melodramatic impact of the plot is centered upon the beautiful dead woman, Marion's wife and Sophy's mother. Cassandra is fascinated by the long-dead Violet and listens to the servants talking about her. Nanny, not unlike Mrs. Danvers in *Rebecca,* takes pleasure in bringing Cassandra to the edge of despair about Violet, with the evocations of her beauty, elegance, and gaiety. As a result, Cassandra, deeply aware of her own insignificance, indulges in gloomy speculations: " 'The chief obstacle he hides,' Cassandra thought, seeing the ghost of Violet, palely coloured like her name. 'That is the only real obstacle between us, the only one which will be there for ever and ever, and scares me and threatens me—his memories of her perfection, in the light of which I shall always fail' " (226–27).

Elizabeth Taylor's way of dealing with melodrama is extremely traditional. A violent death is needed to bring the book to its end. Taylor kills Sophy off, therefore causing the final climax. Sophy's death, although heavily dramatic, is handled in a sober, even abrupt, manner:

She clasped one of the grey goddesses, her thin arms quick and alive against the rain-pitted stone, her yellow dress fluttering. . . .
   In a dreamlike way the statue appeared to move. It reeled drunkenly and Tom stood frozen in a world where things happened beyond his understanding. Cassandra screamed, her hands clapped over her face.
   Tom was strong. He soon lifted the bulk of broken stone, but Sophy, of course, was dead. (184–85)

Since Sophy was not Marion's daughter, but Tom's, she had to be eliminated as the living consequence of the classical triangle situation. It might also have been an attempt on Taylor's part to annihilate the memory of the dead woman, which would give her heroine a chance and give credibility to her own story. No reassurance, however, comes at the end for Cassandra, apart from the knowledge that Marion wants to marry her. The quick dismissal of the child does not solve anything, only adds to the uneasiness felt by the reader regarding the handling of the plot.

Palladian is a disappointing novel which leaves the reader feeling uneasy. The variety of its sources, the awkward handling of the plot and characters, and the heavy melodramatic content make the reader wonder about the author's purpose in writing it. A reviewer once wrote: "Here as in *At Mrs. Lippincote's* we enjoy a fresh talent, a keen ear, a sensitive spirit. . . . But Mrs. Taylor's studied lack of emotion leads neither to hope nor despair. The almost deceitful simplicity of composition cannot compensate for the weakness of motivation. The reader, always conscious of the author's literary gift, will hopefully await its more mature unfolding."[8]

The contrast between the two novels shows two facets of Elizabeth Taylor as a writer. In *At Mrs. Lippincote's,* she appears as a contemporary writer who could have an impact on the postwar British novel. In *Palladian,* she retreats into the past, in the tradition of Elizabeth Bowen and Ivy Compton Burnett. Never, in her later works, will these two aspects of Taylor's fiction be so clearly marked. Never will she appear, so strikingly, as a novelist caught between two widely divergent currents. Her choice will prove to be a compromise between the two worlds, an attempt at being a contemporary novelist while her background, education, and tastes direct her in what we might well call the opposite direction.

Chapter Three

The Creation of a Fictional World

Elizabeth Taylor's next two novels, *A View of the Harbour,* published in 1947, and *A Wreath of Roses,* published in 1949, show a marked evolution in her career. The two novels owe their importance to the fact that, for Taylor, they are further experiments in the field of the novel. In a sense, *At Mrs. Lippincote's* broke away from tradition whereas *Palladian* seemed a prudent retreat into the past. The next two novels are definite attempts at the creation of a fictional world. Taylor sets a mood of her own—a mood of deep nostalgia—the first intimations of which were perceptible in *Palladian.* She also infuses her novels with her latent pessimism which is to become her tradesmark. In an effort to assert herself further as a novelist, Taylor also acknowledges her debt to Virginia Woolf: both novels deal with perception and the vision of the artist, and attempt to give permanence to special "moments of being." In both books, Elizabeth Taylor displays a Woolf-like concern with composition, and even though the two novels do not attain the final form which will establish her reputation as a postwar novelist, they nevertheless appear as significant steps in her evolution.

A View of the Harbour

A View of the Harbour may not be Elizabeth Taylor's most famous novel, but it is undoubtedly one of her most finely written and closely plotted books, "not only a subtly observant study but a highly original narrative."[1] It has also been described as a "gentle and continuous dance in very slow motion, very agreeable to observe, without being the least dramatic."[2] The story revolves around a simple plot. Bertram Hemingway, a retired Navy officer, comes to the little harbor of Newby to paint marine landscapes. An inquisitive old man with a genius for insinuating himself, Bertram soon becomes acquainted with a handful of local characters: old Mrs. Bracey, the local gossip, who is fortunately confined to her bed; Robert Cazabon, the doctor; his wife Beth, a novelist; their two daughters, Prudence and Stevie. Next to the Cazabons lives the pretty Tory Foyle, Beth's closest friend and a divorcée. The novel describes the daily life of this handful of characters during a long summer, soon after the war. Bertram discovers that the lovely Tory, whom he greatly admires, is in fact in love with her best friend's husband, Dr. Cazabon. The classic love-triangle situation is ultimately resolved by Tory's decision to marry Bertram and to move to London with him.

Elizabeth Taylor establishes an interesting parallel between two acts of creation. The story unfolds as Bertram tries to paint a picture of the harbor while Beth tries to finish a novel. Taylor's vision of the artist's predicament is cynical, yet she sympathizes with Bertram's failure to express himself through his paintings and with Beth's inability to grasp reality through her novels. In this third novel, however, there are ironic undertones to the conflict between perception and reality. Taylor's description of artists is highly ironical. She mercilessly mocks both Bertram and Beth.

The title, *A View of the Harbour,* suggests various experiences of perception which cannot, however, be shared. Bertram's idiosyncratic view is colored by his basic optimism which makes him see the harbor as "shimmering with light," whereas another artist translated his own vision into "brown gravy." " 'We see with our souls,' Bertram said sententiously. 'And what we reveal in our paintings is the soul of man, not a mere row of buildings.' Standing in front of Mr. Walker's picture, he felt complacently that Mr. Walker's soul did not come off too well, looked dingily out from behind the gravy-like paint."[3]

Bertram is presented as a failed artist. Occasionally indulging in self-deception, he comforts himself with the thought that many famous men started late in life. His ambition pursues him relentlessly and he keeps seeing in his mind "a dazzling little marine study by Bertram Hemingway," yet when he gets to work "the greens became mud, the birds suggested no possibility of movement, stuck motionless above the waves, the crests of the waves

themselves would never spill" (5). For a while, he attempts
to convince himself that he has talent, searching for other media,
seeing Tory as a muse. However, he finally realizes his limitations. The painting which he leaves behind, unsigned after all,
is barely adequate. The view of the harbor is identifiable, but
not the time of day: "In fact, the very thing I most hoped to
do I have failed over" (327).

If Taylor displays mild irony in describing Bertram's failure
to create a work of art, her attitude toward Beth strikes the
reader as more ambiguous. Beth provides an original and refreshing insight into literary creation. By describing a novelist
much like herself, Taylor offers an ironic insight into the writer's
plight. The portrayal of Beth may, in fact, be a caricature. Supposedly witty and observant, she is described by her own daughter "as blind as a bat" and as "never having made a joke in
her whole life." She is so involved in her little world that she
hardly pays any attention to her children. When debating a
serious problem with her friend, she stops to ponder on the
use of a word, the place of a preposition, or the accuracy of a
simile.

Beth's situation is also presented as deeply ironical. Taylor
insists that human nature, for Beth, is an open book "which,
moreover, she would finish writing herself" (186). Yet she is
the most easily deceived character in the novel. The perception
she is supposed to possess to an extreme degree is entirely concentrated upon her fictional world. Everything she sees, hears,
or feels is translated into fiction. She remains totally blind to
her daughter's difficulties and to her husband's withdrawal. Her
friend Tory cannot help despising her, at times, for her complete
lack of perception, her failure to grasp the tricky situation.

Taylor mocks Beth's insistence on describing scenes which
she has never witnessed—funerals in particular. Plagued by the
fear that her books might be thought frivolous, Beth writes
"funereal, macabre" novels. Although brave and daring in her
fictional world, she is shy and timid in real life.

In spite of her ironical treatment, Taylor deals with Beth
kindly. Even in moments when Beth's total inability to run her
life is described somewhat sarcastically, the reader may feel the
sympathy which Taylor feels for her protagonist. In moments
of truth, also, when Taylor makes Beth say, "I am not a great

writer. Whatever I do someone else has always done it before, and better" (117), the reader may feel Taylor stepping in.

A View of the Harbour is the first novel in which Elizabeth Taylor presents a coherent fictional world. She chooses to isolate her characters in a small world where, without interference from the larger, objective "London" world, they are free to work out their problems with each other. Taylor's choice of setting reflects her desire for a self-contained society. The story takes place in Newby, an old-fashioned little harbor described as "dingy and familiar, a row of buildings, shops, café, pub, with peeling plaster of apricot and sky-blue" (3). This little harbor, cut off from the rest of the world, appears sordid to most of the residents, yet picturesque to the artists. Once a popular resort, it has been deserted in favor of a new town "round the point" where tourists marvel at the implantation of an ice-cream parlor, a cinema, and other modern conveniences. The action takes place soon after the war, although very little is said about the exact timing. The parenthetical remark "(there had been a war on)" reminds one strongly of Virginia Woolf who uses similar devices in *To the Lighthouse,* almost ironical in their concision. There is a little talk about war widows and women officers. Yet Taylor develops a lingering nostalgia for the prewar years bathed in a golden light and symbolized in everyone's mind by the memory of the man with the pink and white striped blazer who used to play at concert parties.

Having clearly limited herself to the old part of the little harbor—a significant choice—Taylor is going to restrict herself further. She only concerns herself with the first row of houses, a device likely to give a two-dimensional aspect to the setting of the novel. She presents the waterfront, where a handful of people live next to each other, as a stage. Next to the large house at one end is the pub, then the Mimosa fish café, the secondhand clothes shop, the Fun Fair, the Seamen's Mission, the Waxworks, the lifeboat house. Between the big square house and the pub there stands a narrow house where most of the action takes place. Beyond the first row of houses, however, the novelist does not venture. This choice of setting does much to convey an impression of isolation, of "monde clos." It also allows Taylor to display her particular skill in characterization. In a closed world, with only a handful of characters, Taylor

has the opportunity to study in depth their individuality and
the connections between them. One critic notes: "Only the nim-
ble fingers of the author manipulate the little figures with skill,
a kind of remote tenderness, which makes of the whole something elusively meaningful and wistfully bright."[4]

Taylor's restricted setting, her closed case study of an odd
medley of characters is, on the whole, very successful. She centers her psychological plot on Tory, presented as a pretty and
intelligent, yet frivolous, woman who has been abandoned by
her husband. It is never made quite clear whether Tory still
loves her husband or whether her pride alone is suffering. The
same ambiguity hovers over her relationship with Robert, Beth's
husband. Robert shows a certain amount of insight:

How does a woman suddenly become aware of a man she has known
for twenty years? No, let *me* tell *you* the answer. Isn't it because
your husband has gone, so that for the first time in your life you
are alone and hate it, and must have some man, because your sort
of woman does have to? And *I* am the man because I am available,
the man who never interested you before, who was merely the boring
creature your friend had unaccountably married. (172–73)

Taylor, who is always discreet in her treatment of characters
and resorts to hints and implications, still manages to convey
a strong impression about Tory, whom she describes as vain
and selfish, with a frivolous attitude toward life in general and
love in particular. When Robert confesses his love for her, Tory
makes desultory comments: " 'I don't think we are going to
get much fun out of this,' she added. 'Fun!' Robert echoed,
rather taken aback by this novel way of looking at serious passion. 'My God! I wouldn't jeopardize the whole of my life,
let all my sense of right be overthrown for mere fun.' 'Oh, I
would,' Tory said" (170).

In spite of Tory's lightheartedness—a mood that tends to
pervade the whole book—Taylor allows her reader to glimpse
the underlying burden her characters bear. The relationship
between Tory and Bertram, whom she finally agrees to marry,
is indicative of two lonely individuals who hope to ward off
loneliness together. A critic notes of Taylor: "Like the retired
commander, who plays the central rôle in the story, she insinu-

ates herself into people's lives and troubles. She lays them bare but with the artist's eye, not the analyst's scalpel, and with the poet's evocative touch."[5] By isolating her characters, Taylor can lay bare, not their "vice and folly" as contemporary satirists would, but rather their deeply rooted loneliness. Taylor wrote: "I think that loneliness is a theme running through many of my novels and short stories, the different ways in which individuals can be isolated from each other. . . ."[6]

All the characters in the novel fight an overwhelming loneliness and their plight is viewed as tragic. Bertram lives by himself, aimlessly. Tory cannot bear the ticking of clock in her deserted house. Prudence spends her time with her cat. Robert Cazabon lives only for his work. Lily Wilson, a young widow, spends her life in terror and desolation. Each of them reacts differently to the pressure of loneliness. Bertram likes to make himself indispensable to others, to make them emotionally dependent on him, which soon tires him and makes him leave them. Tory, when the loneliness overwhelms her, goes to London and buys herself hats. Lily Wilson, desperately seeking sympathy, gets into the habit of going to the pub night after night.

Thus, in spite of the light, amused tone that Taylor maintains throughout the novel, *A View of the Harbour* remains highly melodramatic. Underneath the social comedy, there remains a painful dilemma. The friendship between Tory and Beth, who have known each other since their school days, makes any deception appear particularly callous and the love affair between Tory and Beth's husband totally unrealistic. Consequently, Elizabeth Taylor introduces the notion of sacrifice, a melodramatic device which also implies the existence of a moral sense. Although social pressures do not play any part in the novel, Tory knows that, on purely moral grounds, she must renounce her love for her best friend's husband and go away. Yet, Taylor's treatment of melodrama rings an ironical note. " 'I will go miles away and hide myself in a little bed sitting-room and live on my memories. Where I can harm you no more.' She saw herself lying on a chaise-longue, coughing a little, her hands full of camellias" (266). Even though Taylor cannot resist a melodramatic gesture, its introduction is loaded with ambiguity.

The solution offered is not satisfactory. The fact that Bertram and Tory barely know each other, are not suited to each other, and do not have a very high opinion of each other makes Bertram's proposal rather ludicrous. It arouses the reader's disbelief, and causes the ending to be totally unconvincing.

Another melodramatic device which Taylor used is the intangible presence of the obvious solution. Even though it is never clear whether Tory still loves Teddy, her former husband, she is nevertheless still involved with him from a distance. Tory is constantly reminded of Teddy by the sight of a little yacht, similar to the one he used to sail. This yacht is a constant feature in the novel. "Far out, a white-sailed yacht ventured across the smooth stretch of glinting purple" (189). The hypothetical presence of Teddy's yacht adds to the irony of the protagonists' situation. "That little yacht! . . . A picturesque sight. I've noticed it several times of late" (259). In the last scene of the novel, according to the best tradition of melodrama, the yacht finally approaches. Before Teddy comes on shore to find the house empty, for sale, and Tory gone to London, he exclaims: " 'Nothing has changed,' Teddy Foyle thought. . . . Then, with sensations in his heart of both dread and delight, he set off along the curving arm of the harbour wall towards the waterfront" (340).

The ironical content of this last paragraph is hard to bear. It is almost as if Elizabeth Taylor was consciously ridiculing the melodramatic genre by resorting not only to irony but to ambiguity as well, as if she was purposely making fun of her own characters. *A View of the Harbour* may well have the most ambiguous ending of all of Taylor's novels.

Elizabeth Taylor's concern with form is apparent in the experimental composition of the novel. In both *A View of the Harbour* and *A Wreath of Roses,* Taylor shows her allegiance to Virginia Woolf in a variety of ways. In *A View of the Harbour,* she chooses a lighthouse as the pivot of the setting, a focal point in the structure of the novel. Strangely similar to Woolf's lighthouse whose beams coincide with moments of revelation, the lighthouse in *A View of the Harbour* brings to life, in its harsh light, various images of loneliness. Bit by bit it lights up the scene of a drama. Although its sweeping beam seems to bring people together, the darkness which follows makes their isolation more deeply felt.

Taylor's decision to limit herself to a small number of characters, who, moreover, live in a row of cramped houses, has a highly dramatic value. This stagelike setting is never empty for long. Doors open, people come out, walk along the waterfront, enter their own houses, or simply watch the scene out of their windows. "What a perpetual going and coming there is," Bertram exclaims. The waterfront is also viewed from a distance. Bertram watches it from the lighthouse, and a large number of references to the fishing fleet out at sea gives perspective to the scene thus viewed from so many different angles. Nevertheless, the harbor, limited to the waterfront, stands in total isolation.

The limited number of characters, almost Sartrian in its spareness, allows Taylor to emphasize the interaction between them and adds to the dramatic impact of the novel. Taylor also places them under observation from a central character who acts as an omniscient, yet malevolent, God. If Tory is the center of the psychological plot, Mrs. Bracey, the local gossip, is the center of the dramatic action. From her kitchen first, from her window next, Mrs. Bracey sits in judgment. Day after day, she watches: "What Mrs. Bracey could not see was none the less indicated and her imagination was ready to supply the rest" (234). Literarily speaking, Mrs. Bracey is an extremely interesting creation, one of the best in Taylor's fiction. Described as a Rabelaisian gossip who enjoys nothing more than a coarse joke and spicy reading, Mrs. Bracey is also constantly compared to some kind of malevolent deity: "Up at her window, and in some discomfort (for her shoulder, her chest ached), Mrs. Bracey sat in judgment. Guilt she saw, treachery and deceit and self-indulgence. She did not see, as God might be expected to, their sensations of shame and horror . . ." (236). Yet when the old woman's uncomfortable position at the draughty window causes her to catch a fatal case of pneumonia, she is not let off so easily. Taylor develops her character study further by indulging in ironical speculations on the relationship between Mrs. Bracey and her Maker:

He would receive her orders and listen to her explanations (taking them at their face value), but at the same time could be excluded from any shameful thoughts or family quarrels, nor need He soil

His ears listening to any obscenities or what Mrs. Bracey herself euphe-
mistically called "suggestive stories."

When she shut God away she did not imagine Him turning His
thoughts to any others of His flock. It was rather like giving a maid
the afternoon off, except that she imagined Him mooning about, idle,
restless, waiting to return. (279–80)

Mrs. Bracey plays an important part in *A View of the Harbour.*
Not only does she help give the book cohesion, through the
central role that she plays, but she also provides the synthesis
of the novel. Taylor allies, in her, comedy and melodrama. In
a particularly moving scene, the dying old woman, who remembers her childhood, wishes to communicate the nostalgia she
now feels for the happiness she has once known. Bertram, sitting
at her bedside, fails to understand her: " 'in the things that
really matter to us,' she thought, 'we are entirely alone. Especially alone dying!' " (297). These last few words embody, with
fair accuracy, the constant preoccupation of Elizabeth Taylor's
novels.

A Wreath of Roses

If *A View of the Harbour* remains superficially a light and witty
novel, in spite of its tragic undertones, *A Wreath of Roses* is a
much more complex and confusing book. It is also the work
in which Virginia Woolf's influence is most perceptible. The
novel's epigram, a quotation from *The Waves,* alludes to Taylor's
recurring concern: the conflict between perception and reality.
"So terrible was life that I held up shade after shade. Look at
life through this, look at life through that; let there be rose
leaves, let there be vine leaves—I covered the whole street,
Oxford Street, Piccadilly Circus, with the blaze and ripple of
my mind, with vine leaves and rose leaves."

Once again, Elizabeth Taylor delves into the issue of artistic
creation and the predicament of the artist. Her treatment of
this theme is no longer farcical, however. *A Wreath of Roses*
deals earnestly with the vision of the world which the artist
perceives and tries to present. Taylor has woven this basic theme
into a simple plot relating the difficulties experienced by three
women in their relationships with each other and with outsiders.

The novel becomes confusing, however, when Taylor attempts to integrate these two elements into a mystery plot. This wealth of material tends to blur the message of the novel.

A Wreath of Roses is a novel in which very little happens. Camilla, who is in her thirties and works as a secretary in a girls' school, goes to spend her summer vacation with her long-time friend Liz, at Frances's, who is Liz's former governess. Frances, now a painter, lives in a quiet English village. During the train journey Camilla witnesses a suicide, and this grim event throws her together with a handsome traveler named Richard Elton. Camilla's vacation this year proves to be different from the previous summers. Her companions have changed: Liz is trying to adjust to being a mother; Frances is going through grave doubts about her conception of life, and about the vision she is presenting in her work. Feeling disillusioned about Liz and their broken friendship, Camilla turns to the enigmatic Richard Elton. As the mystery surrounding Richard unravels itself, Camilla realizes how close to tragedy her foolishness has brought her. She is rescued "in extremis" by Morland Beddoes, a great admirer of Frances's paintings, come to precipitate events and bring the story to a close.

By including once again a painter among her characters, Elizabeth Taylor shows her renewed determination to concern herself with the artist's "duty" to the world. Unlike the slightly ludicrous Bertram in *A View of the Harbour,* Frances is presented as a kind of visionary or seer. Taylor uses her largely as a vehicle for her own conception of life, the darkest so far. Frances is going through a crisis—new beliefs clashing with her old ones. She once could paint a girl "as only God, I should have thought, could ever possibly have seen her."[7] She saw life through a pink mist of love and charity. Gradually, though, over the few months preceding the beginning of the story, she comes to the painful realization that she has been misled, that she has sinned against what Virginia Woolf succinctly describes as "suffering; death; the poor" by ignoring them.[8] Where she saw beauty and goodness, at the core of life itself, she now uncovers ugliness and evil. She therefore sets upon the destructive task of canceling her previous work. Now engaged in paying her final tribute to the darker side of life, she accuses herself: "I committed a grave sin against the suffering of the world by ignoring it, by tempting others with charm and nostalgia until they ignored it too" (162). Frances has also changed physically. Now older and in poor health, she knows that she has come to the end of her work. Feeling ashamed of what she revered before—shape in chaos, a pattern in the outside world—she now paints from an inner darkness. Her new vision is the antithesis of the old one which was permeated with charm: "An English sadness like a veil over all I painted, until it became ladylike and nostalgic, governessy, utterly lacking in ferocity, brutality, violence. Whereas in the centre of the earth, in the heart of life, in the core of even everyday things, is there not violence, with flames wheeling, turmoil, pain, chaos?" (42).

Her new vision thus characterized by violence and ferocity, Frances alters her outward behavior as drastically. Pervaded by a strange fierceness, she now plays the piano very loudly, a great confusion of sounds reflecting her inner turmoil; she has added a big fierce dog to the household. When she is ready to show Morland Beddoes her latest four pictures, she confesses: "They reject all that you cared for. I don't want you to feel—dismissed" (164). As she uncovers the pictures, Morland finds himself confronted by what Taylor describes as "the white bones of the earth and dark figures scurrying against a violet sky" (166).

The novel describes Frances's struggle to reconcile herself to her new beliefs, while Morland Beddoes, who believes in her earlier vision, tries to win her back to a more compassionate conception of life. Viewed as the devil come to tempt Frances, Beddoes apparently wins. The outcome is one last painting described as a "creamy-pink-and-yellow picture, half a mirror with reflected hands lifting a wreath of roses, a flash of golden hair" (228). The wreath of roses, a well-known symbol of love, is to be surrendered in a gesture similar to Ophelia's, the last renunciation before death. Yet Frances never completes her work; she turns the unfinished painting to the wall, her last gesture before leaving the studio forever. Thus for Frances, unlike for Lily Briscoe, "the great revelation had never come."[9]

If the last note rings sour, Taylor conveys the idea, nevertheless, that Frances's last gesture is a victory in her fight against reality for, all her life, she had held up "shade after shade." Only when death comes near does she manage to look at life through her naked eyes, the ultimate painful revelation. Taylor therefore implies that Frances's earlier vision was a fraud, that beauty always hides ugliness, that underneath goodness lies evil. Camilla is also used to emphasize Taylor's conviction: " 'When you were a child did you ever hunt for a lost ball among ferns and leaves and, parting them quickly to look—' she made a gesture of doing this '—come suddenly upon a great toad sitting there, very ugly and watchful? All the time there, though you didn't know it, under the leaves. The shock, the recoil!' " (32). At the end of the novel, when Camilla also comes to grips with reality, she makes a similar remark: "Parting the leaves to look for treasure, love, adventure, she inadvertently disclosed evil, and recoiled" (239–40).

The same grimness pervades the relationships between the three women. *A Wreath of Roses* also focuses on human isolation and on the different ways in which to fight loneliness. The characters in the novel are four lonely people who try to evade loneliness each in their own way: Frances through art, Liz through motherhood, Camilla through friendship, Richard through fantasy. Taylor describes their efforts and constant failure to relate to one another. "We are like two people on the opposite sides of a river, and though we strain our voices they cannot carry from one bank to the other" (147).

Once again, the story is told mostly through the consciousness of a woman: Camilla. Camilla is a credible literary creation, yet she appears weak by comparison with Taylor's other heroines. Brought up in the twenties in a stuffy Cambridge home, "in a man's world," Camilla suffers from all the neuroses associated with such a background. She is not a free spirit, as Julia Davenant was, and she envies her friend Liz's warm, loving disposition.

Taylor describes Camilla as the archetype of an empty existence. Her friend Liz, from whom Camilla feels estranged, is now a mother. Taylor contrasts the two women's lives. As a wife and mother, Liz appears fulfilled whereas Camilla bitterly senses her own inadequacy and sees her life as sterile and empty. Liz has her child, Frances has her paintings. " 'And I,' she thought at last, bitterly, 'the physical life, the artistic life, all creativeness closed to me, am left to do the washing-up' " (23). Camilla finds herself facing a severe identity crisis. "A fear of being left out inspired her, a feeling that life was enriching everyone but herself, that education had taken the place of experience, and conversation the place of action" (53). In a desperate attempt to assert herself and to give a sense of direction to her life, she strikes up a dubious friendship with the strange man she has just met, even though she paradoxically despises him. Her behavior toward him is consequently ambiguous: She behaves in a challenging, familiar manner, which is totally unlike herself and for Liz's sole benefit. (25). While being aware that Richard is not her type of man, although her imagination tends to lead her astray, Camilla nevertheless tries to play her role, willing to cast off her old self. Her relationship with Richard is doomed from the start mainly because of her motives: "Her motive at first—but she had forgotten it already—had been to show off to Liz, to deny her own virginity, to punish her for the baby and all the physical experience it symbolized" (89). She intends to prove that she can handle Richard without any shattering aftermath, without breaking the delicate pattern of her life while enriching it with the excitement of romance. " 'Something against next term is what I want,' Camilla thought, staring at the eyes in the mirror. 'Something against the long winter, if only a memory. Not to have to re-enter the school with its bleak cleanness, its smells of paint and polish, with everything in me the same as when I left it, nothing added or taken away, nothing to remember and nothing to look forward to' " (136).

A sense of failure also weighs on Taylor's second heroine, Liz. Liz's warm, impulsive, unpredictable nature is severely checked by her husband's cold, pompous, affected disposition. Her diatribe against marriage, "Marriage is such a sordid, morbid relationship," is only halfhearted, nevertheless. There is, throughout the novel, an exaltation of marriage presented as the only relationship worth experiencing. Liz also feels torn between her loyalty to her husband and her friendship for Camilla whose possessiveness she fears. When Camilla sarcastically questions Arthur's love for his wife, Liz answers: " 'You hope he doesn't,' she said slowly. Her voice was dull and quiet and did not express the enormity of this discovery, nor match her unsteady breathing, nor her frown. 'You hate him so much you hope he doesn't care for me' " (106).

Taylor's last heroine, Frances, is also shown as fighting deep despondency. Although a typical governess and spinster, Frances is a great advocate of relationships. Looking back upon her life, she admits: "Yet I was too self-sufficient, as if I evaded the pain and the delight of human relationships, which I never did knowingly. But if I was ever gravely at fault, I was at fault over that. For even Liz's marriage is better than no marriage at all" (206). Thus she feels veneration for Arthur, Liz's husband, who plays an important part in her fantasy world, and does not understand Camilla's aggressivity toward him. She notes: "But I felt tenderness for people, and love. Hid it, though, with my prim ways as soon Camilla will, and from the same motives: fear and pride" (138–39). Seeing Camilla as an "alter ego," Frances tries to warn her, to show her the pitfalls of the path she is taking: "You are the one I worry for, not Liz. . . . Because you never cry. Because you are so heavily armoured that if you get thrown you'll never rise to your feet again without assistance" (76).

In spite of the grimness that pervades Taylor's description of her women, she conveys much sympathy toward them and never ridicules them. Yet she does not treat her men characters as well as her women. Richard is presented as vain, shallow, and stupid; Arthur as self-infatuated, stuffy, and insensitive; Morland Beddoes as fat, untidy, "absurd and tripperish." Yet Morland Beddoes' vital role in the novel is twofold. First, he is Frances's counterpart, "the devil come to tempt [her]." Since he has built his whole life around her vision of simplicity and love, he fights to make her reconsider her new outlook which, unknowingly, he repudiates as one of pride. Even before he sees Frances's latest pictures, he exclaims: "I hate those great agonized pictures which say 'I,' 'I,' all the time. 'I am crucified.' 'I suffer' " (162). Morland Beddoes also plays the part of the detective, endowed with kindness and compassion, who unravels the mystery surrounding Richard Elton and rescues Camilla when she finally breaks down.

The mystery plot in *A Wreath of Roses* is the least satisfactory element of the novel, although Taylor attempts to keep to the conventions of the genre and manages to sustain a certain amount of suspense. While Morland Beddoes is cast in the part of the rescuer whose presence also precipitates events, Richard

Elton plays the part of the mystery man soon discovered to be the villain. Richard, who is described as "an unlikely man," is indeed a thin literary creation. A good-looking man, a philanderer, he is characterized by a curious emptiness of expression. In the most dramatic moments, when Camilla turns to look into his eyes, she sees nothing but blankness. Elizabeth Taylor describes him as a mythomaniac who cannot deal with reality and confesses: "I can't tell what is real any longer" (198). At times, however, Richard seems capable of lucidity toward himself: "He did not know which was real. He had always told lies, always invented sources of self-pity. If he had an audience, he was saved. When he was alone he was afraid. He had banished reality, and now it was as if he were only reflected back from the mirrors of other people's minds" (183).

Taylor expands the mystery element by including excerpts from Richard's diary and by describing Camilla's increasing involvement with him, as well as Morland Beddoes's growing watchfulness. The ending, however, is not much of a surprise. The final horror for Camilla comes at the close of the novel when, to find shelter from the rain, Richard takes her to a deserted house. She then discovers that he is a psychopath who feeds on violence. Camilla escapes in time to save herself and abandons him to his own fate.

The mystery plot could have safely been left out without weakening in the least the rest of the novel. Its absence would have avoided confusion and made the novel richer. It seems that Taylor attempted too much and lost in the process some of her usual brilliance.

Yet, overall, the novel retains its cohesion through its clever structure, circular as a wreath. The plot forms a complete circle, starting with a death and ending with a death, both suicides committed in the same manner. These two deaths provide a pattern that preserves the wholeness of the book. The train, another constant in the novel, is not shown as traveling along a straight line, but around an imaginary circle. When she watches the train plodding along the valley, Liz remarks: "It will never get anywhere" (209). Camilla, traveling by train, looks out of the window and notices "the same deserted platform, the geraniums—as if they had completed a circle" (7). Taylor uses the image to stress once again the uselessness of all human purposes, the vanity of men's efforts.

In spite of a certain amount of confusion, *A Wreath of Roses* remains a remarkable book. One critic notes: "It is her sense of innumerable momentary understandings that pleases."[10] Nothing reminds one more strongly of Virginia Woolf than Taylor's attempts at giving permanence to the moment. Her descriptive skill, which seems to have all the characteristics attributed to Frances's early paintings, illustrates the connection between the two novelists: "The sunlight coming in diamonds through the lace curtains chequered and broke up the picture of her, flashed in the wine, spilt over the carpet, and revealed the tawny wreaths lying on the pink. Gold dust drifted upwards through the imprisoned sunshine, but nothing else moved . . ." (105). It is those special moments, which Woolf would describe as "little daily miracles, illuminations, matches struck unexpectedly in the dark,"[11] that Taylor excels at depicting, the effort to make life stand still for just a moment: "Afternoons seem unending on branch-line stations in England in summer-time. The spiked shelter prints an unmoving shadow on the platform, geraniums blaze, whitewashed stones assault the eye. Such trains as come only add to the air of fantasy, to the idea of the scene being symbolic, or encountered at one level while suggesting another even more alienating" (3). Elizabeth Taylor, however, cannot endorse Virginia Woolf's conviction that "In the midst of chaos, there was a shape; this eternal passing of flowing . . . was struck into stability."[12] *A Wreath of Roses* is a pessimistic novel revealing a dispirited vision of life. Taylor dissociates herself from Woolf's more positive outlook.

"Life's not simplicity," she said slowly. "Not loving-kindness either. It's darkness and the terrible things we do to one another and to ourselves. The sooner we are out of it the better. And paintings don't matter. They are like making daisy-chains in the shadow of a volcano. Pathetic and childish. . . .

The only thing that makes sense of it all is looking up at the sky at night and knowing that even the burden of cruelty we have laid upon the earth scarcely exists, will fly away into dust, is nothing, too infinitesimal to matter." (163)

Even though Taylor's beliefs are never so clearly asserted in any other novel, they remain a constant feature of her fiction.

Both *A View of the Harbour* and *A Wreath of Roses* appear as
landmarks in Taylor's work. They are the two initial novels
from which her later work will largely derive. While *A View
of the Harbour* displays her ability to depict, with great wit, various aspects of social interplay, *A Wreath of Roses* reveals a deeper
and darker side of her personality—her basic pessimism and
lack of faith in human nature. Both are original novels showing
great individuality. More importantly, they are united by the
author's clear intention to create a coherent fictional world.
The link between the two novels is made apparent in an exchange between two characters in *A Wreath of Roses*. Looking
down from the top of a hill at the little town in which they
are staying, they remark:

> "It has a life of its own," he said, and he swept his hand across
> the scene. "It is a corporate thing, with its own atmosphere, its own
> set of characters. It breeds its own set of characters, as Rouen bred
> Madame Bovary. I can imagine tragedy down there, and drama. I
> can imagine an English Madame Bovary and the old ladies in the
> tea-shops watching her, the men in the pubs lifting their mouths from
> their mugs as she passes in the street. . . ."
> "It is what they call a slice of life," Arthur agreed. "A town like
> that runs across England from the highest to the lowest. . . ." (209–
> 10)

Taylor's determination to create her "own atmosphere" breeding "its own set of characters" will become increasingly obvious
in her following novels and will soon set her apart from her
contemporary fellow novelists.

Chapter Four

The Flight into Fantasy

In most of her novels, Elizabeth Taylor describes the difficulties that her characters experience in coming to terms with reality. *Angel* and *The Sleeping Beauty,* however, are set apart in Taylor's fiction by their emphatic refusal to deal with the reality of the outside world. The characters in both novels are shown as escaping into a world of fantasy of their own making. *Angel,* a fascinating study in self-deception, is a chronicle of the rise and fall of an Edwardian novelist who suffers from delusions of grandeur. *The Sleeping Beauty* displays an obdurate wish, on the part of its protagonist, to see life as a fairy tale. In both novels, the attempts made to revert to reality fail. As the story lines show little bearing on reality, it is difficult to ascertain what Taylor's intentions were; consequently, both novels are flawed by a certain amount of ambivalence.

Angel

Elizabeth Taylor's seventh novel, *Angel,* published in 1957, received warm critical applause. Described as "something of a new departure,"[1] the new novel both surprised and delighted critics who hailed a new facet of Taylor's talent and praised her versatility. For the first time, Taylor deals with a whole life span, instead of a few weeks, as in her previous novels. Her study of Angel Deverell starts in 1900 when she is fifteen, and ends with her death shortly after the end of World War II. The book is divided into six sections. The first three relate Angel's slow rise to fame, from the drabness of the little shop in Norley to her luxurious house in Alderhurst, and the apex of her fame and eccentricity in London. The last three sections describe her brief married life, her gradual loss of popularity, and her slow and inexorable decline. The tone of the novel is also different from that of Taylor's previous work. Whereas her earlier novels charmed her readers by the quietness of their tone, *Angel* shocks them by its stridency. Far from describing good behavior, moderation and taste, Taylor now deals with absurdity, outrageousness and vulgarity. She does so no longer with reverence and compassion, but with what Kingsley Amis describes as "spendid relish" and "contemptuous charity."[2] For the first time, Taylor also displays a form of antifeminism. Her three main characters—Angel Deverell, Nora Howe-Nevinson, and Lady Baines—are portrayed with pitiless irony. Angel is presented as eccentric, arrogant, and self-absorbed, while Nora is described as a fastidious self-made martyr, and Lady Baines as an extravagant nouveau riche. Taylor's sympathy seems to be largely directed to her male characters, especially Theo Gilbright, Angel's publisher, who appears lucid and compassionate. Esmé, Angel's husband, is described as superficial and untrustworthy, yet rational and clear-minded. At last, Marvell, Angel's gardener and chauffeur, if slovenly and lazy, appears kind and faithful.

The novel nevertheless retains some of the characteristics of Taylor's earlier work. It still deals not so much with loneliness as with isolation. The characters, once again, find themselves in a closed world; this time, however, the isolation is engineered by Angel's personality, by her obstinate refusal to deal with the outside world. Angel's loneliness is felt acutely: "I am quite alone and there is no hope, she thought."[3] Her suffering is paradoxical for she cannot relate to those around her. "She faced and suffered her solitariness; braved out the agony of longing she now felt for someone to be sitting beside her to whom she could communicate her bitter loneliness" (49–50).

If this first appeal for compassion and sympathy seems a little sterotyped—it is after all a leitmotiv in Taylor's fiction—Angel's burden soon becomes more apparent and therefore convincing. Esmé understands the paradox of her loneliness that is at the root of the romantic fantasies which Angel writes, yet also results both from the act of creation and the ensuing fame. When he paints her portrait, at her request, he chooses to portray her as he perceives her "in her darkest clothes against a banal background; the empty window behind her, the bare wall, emphasised the suggestion of loneliness. He had been tempted to scrawl a title upon the blank side of the canvas: 'Study in Solitary

Confinement' " (138). Even at the apex of her career, Angel's arrogance and eccentricity cut her off from the rest of the world. Therefore, when her fame dies out, she finds herself totally alone. At the end of the novel, sick Angel braves a snowstorm to go and see her gardener, Marvell. Her friend Nora is appalled by the unreasonableness of her action: " 'Whatever possessed you?' 'I felt lonely,' said Angel and the words surprised herself" (245). Thus, her loneliness proves to be the cause of her death, a grim version of Taylor's recurring theme.

Besides its concern with loneliness, a preoccupation which can be viewed as Taylor's trademark, the most striking feature about *Angel* remains the protagonist's refusal to deal with reality and her consequent flight into fantasy. If, unlike most of Taylor's heroines who struggle to accept reality, Angel dismisses it completely, the story line also betrays a certain taste for fantasizing. Taylor conveys an impression of unreality both about Angel's way of dealing with life and about the way life deals with her. At the beginning of the story, Angel is presented as an obscure young girl who has neither wit, nor beauty, nor charm, nor education. What she possesses to an extreme degree is imagination, vanity, and a fair amount of vulgarity. She writes "vulgarly over-written" novels, full of improbabilities and inaccuracies. As a result, Angel's overnight success appears somewhat ambiguous, for she seems, by all accounts, a bad writer. Taylor does nothing to dispel the ambiguity of her heroine's situation when she gleefully describes Angel's unshakable belief in her own genius and her consequent outrageous behavior.

The novel may best be described as a study in self-deception. Angel, who is presented as a "romantic narcissistic woman," cannot accept the slightly sordid facts of her early life. She wishes to forget her humble origins, the little shop and the two rooms above it, the dirty street with its malt smell from the close-by brewery. The fact that she is neither good-looking, nor famous, nor rich, nor brilliant seems a personal affront to her. As she is frightened by the stark reality of her life, she learns to reject all the facts from her past, to triumph over the threatening truth.

At other times she was menaced by intimations of the truth. Her heart would be alarmed, as if by a sudden roll of drums, and she would spring to her feet, beset by the reality of the room, her own face—not beautiful she saw—in the looking glass and the commonplace sounds in the shop below. She would know then that she was in her own setting and had no reason for ever finding herself elsewhere; know moreover that she was bereft of the power to rescue herself, the brains or the beauty by which other young women made their escape. Her panic-stricken face would be reflected back at her as she struggled to deny her identity, slowly cosseting herself away from the truth. She was learning to triumph over reality, and the truth was beginning to leave her in peace. (15)

Angel feels the need to forge a new identity for herself. Unable to accept her humble origins, she starts making up stories about her birth. She recklessly hints at illegitimacy, foreign blood. "My infancy seems to have been wrapped in mystery. Brought to Norley at a very young age I certainly was; but from where, I cannot discover. My mother's reticence hides some old grief and I would not, for that reason, question her or ask about my father, whom I never saw" (104–5). As Angel is incapable of moderation, the new identity she creates for herself is flamboyant. Portraits of ancestors on the walls of a rented apartment she immediately makes hers. Her friend Nora becomes alarmed by the magnitude of the lies: "Then even grander notions followed and contradicted the first, and Nora, with her heart full of love and understanding, saw the lies as a pathetic necessity, an ingredient of genius, a part of the make-believe world from which the novels came" (121–22).

Angel's world of fantasy betrays a distorted vision of her own life. Taylor stresses her character's idiosyncrasies to the point where roles are reversed: Angel's fictional world becomes reality; her dukes and duchesses—for she deals solely with aristocrats—her only real people. She adopts their values, their prejudices, their way of life. Angel has an equally distorted vision of herself. Her ambiguous success leads her to believe that she is a great novelist, that her contribution to literature will pass the test of time. When her popularity dies out, she stubbornly refuses to accept that her career is over. Poverty, neglect, and starvation do not affect her: "Perhaps she saw nothing as it was, everything as it should be, though doubtless never had been; thought she retained whatever her hands had once touched: fame, love, money" (211).

When Angel finds herself suddenly confronted by reality, she suffers a great shock for she is ill-equipped to deal with its inexorability. Her first discovery of Paradise House, years after she described it in her first novel, totally dumbfounds her: "But how different it was from her dreams and from the house she had described in her first novel. The ashen look of the stone was a great shock to her. It was all built the wrong way about and was not big enough or decorated enough, and there were no peacocks" (146).

On one occasion, Angel's confrontation with truth threatens her whole being. The discovery of a love letter, long after Esmé's death, suddenly undermines the belief that she has fostered in the perfection of her brief marriage. The potential destruction which they foresee alarms her friends to such an extent that they try to protect her. Angel's fight with what she suspects to be the truth, yet what she cannot live with is tragic: "But he could see that there were moments when the facts, as they seemed indisputably to be, leapt at her: the truth took her by the throat; then her hand would fly up to her cheek and her eyes stare. Her suffering at such moments was too sharp to be endured: she could not live with such a kind of truth. With Theo's help and Nora's acquiescence she had begun, oyster-like, to coat over, to conceal what could not be borne as it was" (233).

The same ambiguity, which pervades Angel's life of fame and success, is also perceptible in Taylor's treatment of her character. Angel's name in itself bespeaks of a certain irony. Jokes are made: "Angels ever bright and fair" and "Angel by name and Angel by nature." Yet, Taylor's central character appears as a fallen angel. The portrait of Angel Deverell, which Taylor offers her readers, is pitiless at times. Kingsley Amis once wrote: "Comedy of a special kind—its attachments include a splendid relish and a sort of contemptuous charity—is one of Mrs. Taylor's leading talents."[4] In *Angel,* Taylor displays both sides of her talent, which generates a certain amount of ambiguity and causes some uneasiness in the reader. There is a double standard in *Angel* and Taylor's attitude toward her character is not always clear.

Angel is indeed the first novel in which Taylor betrays a "splendid relish" in her description of a character. Very early in the novel, she sets the mood by the use of a metaphor: "Once he saw a large cactus-plant in a flower-shop window. From one unpromising, barbed shoot had sprung a huge, glowering bloom. It looked solitary and incongruous, a freakish accident; and he was reminded of Angel" (77).

Thus, as a character, Angel is indeed "a really memorable union of the frightful, the comic and the pathetic."[5] The comic aspect results from pushing the frightful to the limit of absurdity. Described as tall, bony, with a harsh voice and an ugly accent, Angel is not an attractive woman. Moreover, her vanity and arrogance are great. At sixteen, she curtly refuses to make any suggested alterations to her crude first novel, *The Lady Irania,* as she cannot imagine her masterpiece in need of being touched up or toned down. To her mother who tries to instill some humility in her, Angel replies: "We may all be equal in the sight of God, as you are always telling me, but we are not all equal in *my* eyes . . ." (84). Socially, she is described as dull and dominating, and is easily recognized "on account of her air of authority and the absurdity of her clothes" (135). Taylor often indulges in mocking descriptions: "She went to the Royal Garden Party in violet satin and ostrich-feathers with purple-dyed chinchilla on her shoulders; amethysts encrusted her corsage and mauve orchids were sewn all over her skirt where they quickly wilted. Glances of astonishment she interpreted as admiration" (122).

Elizabeth Taylor goes a long way to make her heroine appear outrageous. Not unlike other women novelists of the Ouida school, Angel displays neither taste nor moderation. She has a photograph of herself "garbed as one of the muses, sitting on a marble seat in a trance, with her mother standing up behind her at a respectful distance" (78). Regarding the war as a personal affront to her, she decides to ignore it totally, banishing all newspapers from her sight: "The war has separated me from my husband and was the cause of our first disagreement, and I never allow Nora or anyone else to mention it in my presence" (166).

Angel's portrayal is by all means frightful. Yet her character can also be pitiable, for Taylor displays a certain amount of charity, as Amis has noted. There is, however, no evidence that her charity is mingled with contempt. Taylor can play very effectively with the reader's sympathy, and her heroine is occasionally presented as a lonely individual, extremely vulnerable, full of uncertainty and doubts, courageous, loyal, and faithful. Yet the various impressions Taylor tries to convey occasionally clash. There are, at times, contradictions between the way Angel allegedly feels and the way she is made to behave.

It is mostly through her male characters that Taylor expresses the compassion she feels for Angel. Only they, she implies, are aware of her heroine's sensitivity and vulnerability. Angel's greatest advocate is her publisher, Theo Gilbright, who tries to shield her both from the mockeries which her writing breeds and from the heartache of her marriage to faithless Esmé. Taylor switches, sometimes abruptly, from a merciless description of Angel to a sympathetic description of her heroine's feelings. Theo's first meeting with Angel makes a deep impression on him: "Theo saw her pale face glistening, guessed that she had been late and anxious, imagined her walking too quickly through the hot streets" (53).

Through Esmé's consciousness, Angel is presented no longer as a caricature but as a real human being. Esmé is quick to detect Angel's vulnerability: "Love and the wine transformed her. As she was *now* he wanted to paint her—not staring him out in defiance, as she had done, but glowing, uncertain, with thoughts crowding in, some of them, he could tell, disturbing" (133). Soon, however, Angel's courage and loyalty only serve to emphasize Esmé's weakness and treachery. His guilt prevents him from reaching out toward her and they become alienated.

As Angel gets older and the circumstances of her life become grimmer, she is presented as more pathetic. Her gardener Marvell, who also becomes her soul-mate, contributes to provide a compassionate account of her. Taylor describes, with great sympathy, Marvell's reactions to the news of Angel's sickness and impending death:

" 'You've no right out,' I said: 'You know your chest as well as I do.' Now what's she landed herself with? Pneumonia it is, I can tell you, doctor, sir. 'It's pneumonia,' I said, 'and you can take the blame yourself.' 'You've got fussy in your old age,' was what she told me and 'Someone's got to fuss,' I said. The bloody stubbornness of her, and I'll tell her to her face. I'm not one to mince my words with her."

For a moment or two, they pushed their way through the snow in silence. Then Marvell said: "She's as strong as a horse, you know," and tears began to run down his face. (248)

The most striking aspect of Angel's personality which arouses the reader's sympathy is her fear that she has not escaped from poverty after all, that her life has to be lived all over again. As death comes near, all her doubts about herself seem to culminate in an explosion of intense fear. The mask falls, she feels stripped of any identity; panic engulfs her:

If she could understand where she was, she might remember who she was; but she was lost, isolated, without identity. It suddenly occurred to her that she was dead: her heart thundered in her body and Nora felt the sweat trickling down the inside of her arm, running from her wrist into the palm of her hand. Then to Angel it seemed that she was not so much dead as back at the very beginning. It is to be done all over again, she thought. . . .
Nora sponged the sweat from her forehead and then leaned close to her as her lips moved.
"Where are you?" she said gently, as if to a sleepy child. "Why, you are at home, with Nora and naughty Silky Boy, at Paradise House."
The panic lifted. Angel was overwhelmed with relief. She realised that it was not to be gone through again; after all she was at home, in her own bed, with her own life behind her. "I am Angel Deverell," she said and the words were very loud and triumphant and echoed around the room. Nora heard nothing for nothing had been said. (248–49)

Elizabeth Taylor undoubtedly knows how to create pathos. What her reader may find disturbing, however, is the mixture of compassion and sarcasm that fill the pages of the novel. It is difficult to ascertain whether Taylor intends to ridicule Angel or to pity her. The two elements do not blend well, and this leads to a certain amount of ambivalence. Taylor's portrayal of Angel Deverell, which in certain aspects is a masterpiece, also breeds a great deal of uneasiness; unable to decide what Taylor's intentions are, the reader hovers uncertainly between derision and compassion until the last pages.

Angel's most interesting aspect lies in the form of literary parody which the novel contains, and Taylor is particularly virulent in describing her character's literary idiosyncrasies. Angel Deverell, a third-rate writer of romantic fantasies, is a composite portrait of Ouida, Rhoda Broughton, and Marie Corelli. Taylor uses the parallel she establishes between Angel and the once-famous novelists to ridicule a literary genre which has become obsolete.

As she has decided, early in her career, that "experience was an unnecessary and usually baffling obstacle to her imagination," Angel feels no qualms in describing what she has no knowledge of. Taylor pitilessly underlines her heroine's proposterous venture:

"What is the theme of the new book?"
"It is about an actress."
"Are you interested in the theatre, Miss Deverell?"
"I have never been to one."
"Then you are a great reader, perhaps?"
"No, I don't read much. I haven't got any books, and nowadays I am always writing." (54)

Having summarily discarded her limited experience, Angel manages to create out of the sheer power of her imagination. Her fictional world is totally alien to the circumstances of her early life which she wishes to forget. "She escaped from it to her dukes and duchesses, her foreign counts, her castles and moonlit terraces. There were dungeons and crypts and family vaults in her stories, but not cemeteries; the only poor were penniless beggars; and the seaside always was abroad" (76).

Little is said about Angel's novels, apart from some allusions to her confusions of Greek and Roman deities, her high-flown language, and her extravagance. Her prose is described as "ornamental" with "crescendos and alliterations." Taylor does not offer any excerpt of it, only a brief parody of her style. "Kindly raise your corruscating beard from those iridescent pages of shimmering tosh and permit your mordant thoughts to dwell for one mordant moment on us perishing in the corruscating workhouse, which is where we shall without a doubt find ourselves, among the so-called denizens of deep-fraught penury. Ask yourself—nay, go so far as to enquire of yourself—how do we stand by such brilliant balderdash and *live,* nay, not only live but exist too . . ." (51).

Angel's writing experience is described as "trance-like," as a "projection into another world." Her success is said to rest on the magnetic power of her imagination onto unsophisticated readers. G. K. Chesterton once wrote that it was equally impossible not to laugh at Ouida and not to read her; the same could well be said of Angel.

Like Rhoda Broughton, Angel becomes famous for her outspokenness and lack of restraint. She constantly indulges in denunciations and irrelevancies. "Many were shocked by what, in those days, was called 'outspokenness' and by her agnosticism— for in her books only fools and hypocrites were made to believe in God—and to be spoken against once or twice from pulpits had been of some assistance to her" (75).

Like Marie Corelli, Angel is known as being extraordinarily sensitive to any form of criticism. Her morbid hatred for one particular critic, Rowland Pearce, who called her novels "gibberish" induces her to start a revengeful novel.

She would call it "The Charlatan" and it should deal with a literary hack, an impoverished scribbler, a novelist manqué, a twisted and embittered man, making a despicable living by reviling the work of better writers than himself, assuaging his jealousy and impotence by destroying what he could not himself create. She imagined him with the utmost vividness: a misshapen figure of a man, with a stained waistcoat and a sneering voice. He had repulsive personal habits, no friend in the world, and a name as much like Rowland Pearce as she could manage. (70)

Taylor's final judgment on Angel's literary talent is a cool dismissal. After mentioning the fact that Nora gave up writing poetry to facilitate Angel's novel writing, Taylor mockingly adds: "The poetry was lost and the novels were gained, and posterity was as indifferent as it could be about both" (117).

Elizabeth Taylor is at her best when she displays what Kingsley Amis described as "that entrancing spitefulness which, going beyond the merely catty, borders on the tigrine."[6] She can be pitiless, with a gusto which delights critics and readers alike.

Yet, in an effort to create a "round" character instead of a two-dimensional farcical one, or perhaps because of her compulsive compassion toward her protagonist, Taylor feels the need to introduce pathos, a device that tends to create confusion. It never becomes clear whether Taylor intended to write a character study or a satire. The ambivalence of Taylor's split intentions may be the one flaw of an otherwise well-written book.

The Sleeping Beauty

The Sleeping Beauty is a disconcerting and disappointing novel. A reviewer wondered: "What does it all amount to?"[7] The question is not easily answered for the novel lacks purpose. The main character, Vincent Tumulty, supposedly a confirmed bachelor, comes to a small seaside resort to console an old friend, Isabella Godden, after the death of her husband. He falls in love with a beautiful mysterious woman, Emily, who lives a nunlike existence, and tries to win her out of her seclusion. As Vincent's relationship with Emily slowly progresses, inquisitive Isabella discovers that Vincent is already married. Moreover, as his wife refuses to divorce him, Vincent decides to commit bigamy and marry his Sleeping Beauty regardless of the possible consequences.

The plot does not carry conviction. It has been called grotesque, a little harshly yet not quite unjustly. The ending is almost embarrassing: When Emily finally learns the truth about Vinny's past, she remarks: "It is wrong of me, but I begin to admire you more. I didn't know you had this in you. And I admire myself more for bringing it out."[8] The conversation between the newly married couple who cannot bear, out of some inner delicacy, no doubt, to use such words as "bigamy" and "jail," is full of embarrassing circumlocutions: "I should not be there so very long, in the place where I shall never have to go—a few months perhaps." And, "I once heard—years ago, before it had any application to myself—that men who commit—who make this sort of mistake, are the worst treated by the other—by men who have made different mistakes. They are said to resent the tendency in their colleagues and look down on them" (248).

The novel, however, is not about bigamy. Its title, *The Sleeping*

Beauty, suggests a link with the fairy tale, a theme which Elizabeth Taylor wishes to exploit in two different ways: through
Emily and through Vinny. Taylor conveys the idea that Emily's
situation is comparable to that of the Sleeping Beauty. Once a
very attractive, outgoing, mildly promiscuous girl, Emily was
involved in a serious car accident which disfigured her. A sur-
geon managed to re-create her lost beauty but in a totally different manner and, when she first saw her new face in a mirror,
Emily felt lost: "Until then, however in pain, bandaged, in darkness, despairing, I had been myself. But in that looking glass
there was no vestige of me" (171). Emily's particular ordeal
is described as her having lost her sense of self. Her lost identity,
following the physical and psychological shock of the deadly
accident, leaves her under the impression that she is only half
alive. She automatically withdraws from the world and becomes
a recluse. "She felt locked away in herself but ignorant of her
identity, and often she awoke suddenly in the night without
any idea of who she was, thinking firstly that she had died"
(51). At their first meeting, Vinny is struck by the masklike,
terrifying quality of her beauty behind which she shelters. She
has also allowed her apathy to make her the prisoner of her
sister Rose whom Vinny soon recognizes as another obstacle
to overcome: "He thought of Emily lying under the spell of
her alien beauty, and Rose's devotion enclosing her like a thicket
of briers" (48). Described as a zombie because of her lost identity, her lack of determination, and the presence of a jealous
possessive sister, Emily is presented as a great challenge to Taylor's hero.

There is a certain irony in the fact that Taylor casts a middle-
aged underwriter at Lloyd's as the prince of the fairy tale. Yet,
Vinny described as a romantic, because of his emotional integ-
rity, may be the ideal candidate to wake Emily up from her
lethargy. Vinny is a dreamer, a man who sees the past and
the future as real but finds the present "dull, meaningless."
As such, he lives in a dreamworld and has difficulty relating
to reality. He cannot help daydreaming about the mysterious
woman he has barely met. "Having created a personality for
her, and behaviour, and even response, this dream had in a
way presented her to him, given her a voice and words to say"
(31–32). In the tradition of the fairy tale, Emily does not disap-

point Vinny by not fitting the unrealistic mold he has made for her. The flight into fantasy, which the whole relationship emphasizes, is one that Taylor appears to condone, since the two lovers do not seem to have to work their way through either adjustment or disillusionment. Emily, who has in a sense been created by Vinny, is made to exclaim: " 'Oh, I am nothing without you,' she said. 'I should not know what to be. I feel as if you had invented me. I watch you inventing me, week after week' " (187). Emily has little reality outside of Vinny's dreamworld, which supports Taylor's metaphor of the fairy tale.

Like the prince in the tale, Vinny soon becomes aware that he desperately wants to marry Emily. Yet many obstacles stand in his way. Emily's possessive sister Rose has no intention of allowing her sister to revert to her old self and leave her. Vinny's bossy mother shows no inclination to stop controlling her son's life, as she has been doing for the past fifty years. Vinny's wife in name only, Rita, refuses to contemplate a divorce. Meddling Isabella who has ferreted the truth about Vinny's marriage seems intent on informing the interested parties.

At the end of the novel, Taylor weakly reverts to the metaphor of the fairy tale to justify her protagonist's actions: "People who are wakened from a long sleep are exposed to many dangers. The prince in the fairy tale knew that when he wakened the Sleeping Beauty, and he married her the very same day. The difficulties began—they did not end—with his kiss. I am no prince—as you are, very reasonably, waiting to say—but I am not above learning from a fairy tale" (243).

The unlikeliness and weakness of the story line are a great deterrent to admirers of Taylor's fiction. One reviewer writes: "The plot is grotesque: but once it has been accepted, or ignored, there can be little but admiration for the subtlety and humour with which Miss Taylor has invested her whole curious fairy-story."[9] The novel, once again, retains a certain distinction through Taylor's undeniable gift for characterization. For the first time, Taylor centers the action on a male protagonist. Vincent Tumulty is an interesting, well-drawn character whom she describes with perception and great finesse. Close to fifty, Vinny lives with a possessive mother. He is known for his kindness and compassion and offers sympathy whenever the occasion arises: "There's Vinny going in with the wreaths," Isabella has always thought. In everyone's mind, he is associated with condolences and gloom. Vinny is also characterized by a strong desire to be loved. His meeting with Laurence, Isabella's son, shows a revealing effort on his part to take over: "He came forward to shake hands, with the grave and slightly suspicious air of a psychiatrist. Laurence felt the authority, the calm fatherliness, firm yet casual, detached yet compassionate. The brown eyes looked directly at him but veiled Vinny's impressions. The handshake was cordial. 'You are welcome to follow me to the ends of the earth,' Vinny seemed to be assuring people when he was introduced" (12). Laurence's undisguised dislike for him is a source of grief to Vinny, who makes it his business to be loved, "a mission created afresh with everyone he met" (23–24). Laurence sees him as a man who loves putting others under an obligation to him and resents him accordingly.

Taylor's description of Vinny is a caricature at times, especially in the relationship with his mother. By her own admission, Mrs. Tumulty is "mother, father, nurse, wife, godparent, teacher, confessor, psychoanalyst, to him" (101–2). She has trained her son to be a perfect gentleman and constantly expects him to jump to his feet, pull off his hat, give up his chair, and open doors for ladies. Mrs. Tumulty's ascendant on Vinny—in spite of his free spirit—is an interesting notion which Taylor only sketches; nor does she dwell on its possible consequences on the relationship between Vinny and Emily.

Elizabeth Taylor, nevertheless, treats her hero with considerable sympathy. Vinny, who is said to love "charm, grace, discretion, order," seems used, at times, as a vehicle for Taylor's ideas. He once explains to Emily: "Perhaps 'pity' is one of those beautiful and debased words, like 'charity.' Ruined by condescension. If there is condescension, one-sidedness, in it, I couldn't feel it for you" (170). Vinny's sensitivity is shown as a rare gift, for he anticipates his friends' reactions to any given situation and imagines their anguish and their suffering. The combination of imagination and sensitivity is a characteristic which Elizabeth Taylor values greatly.

Next to Vinny's characterization, what saves *The Sleeping Beauty* is the sum of delightful scenes that fill the novel. In spite of the fact that the hero is a man, Taylor's world remains essentially feminine. Through a large use of dialogues, Taylor points out the futility of some idle women's lives. Isabella Godden and her friend Evalie Hobson, described as middle-aged schoolgirls, are presented as self-concerned and frivolous. Almost exclusively interested in their appearances, they spend afternoons at the Turkish baths or at home with mud packs on their faces, indulging in cozy gossiping or discussing their little "flutters" on horses. Following the death of her husband, Isabella has learned to rely on Vinny, whose frequent visits deceive her into thinking that he will eventually propose to her. She constantly rehearses in her mind a kind rejection, yet when she finds out that he is in love with Emily, she feels betrayed. Isabella is never presented as a tragic figure, however; even her fundamental silliness is viewed as a comic trait. Taylor also implies that Isabella's destructive role in unmasking Vinny's masquerade only stems from thoughtlessness, and that there is no malice in her.

Taylor is not always kind to the women she describes. Her portrait of Rose is fairly ruthless. Described as "the most English-looking woman" that Vinny has ever seen, she is shown as being stiff and uncompromising, brisk and always under control. "Such women are a product of English imperviousness and courage, which contain both fanaticism and narrow loyalties. In foreign countries—and Rose seemed so much a soldier's wife—the lack of sensuality was a defense and at times a maddening challenge. The attribute was always jealously fostered and guarded by husbands" (40).

Taylor establishes an interesting parallel between the two sisters Rose and Emily, who grew up with antithetical personalities. Whereas Rose appeared frigid, withdrawn, constantly ailing, Emily was described as warm and promiscuous, healthy and adventurous. Since Emily's accident, which also killed Rose's husband, Rose has finally got control over her destiny as well as her sister's. Behind the love which she professes for Emily, there remains a strong antagonism which makes Rose keep her sister an emotional prisoner. Yet when Emily finds the determination to break free from Rose's clutches to marry Vinny, Rose does little to stop her, as if the spell had indeed been broken.

Taylor paints a very convincing picture of Rose—whom she also uses as a character foil for Emily—by contrasting two dramatically different personalities. Emily, however, remains bland by comparison with sharply individualized Rose. The rivalry between the two sisters is a rich topic which Taylor barely sketches. Rose's quick acceptance of her sister's new situation and Emily's light-hearted dismissal of her sister's plight seem a let-down. The reader may well regret that Taylor did not construct her plot around the two sisters' complex relationship.

Taylor achieves another great success with her characterization of Vinny's mother, Mrs. Tumulty. It is the sharpness with which she creates such secondary characters which makes her fictional world so very lively. She describes Mrs. Tumulty with humor yet with sympathy: "She was deeply in black, though black of such a rustiness and dustiness that it had derived a special texture from its defects. Under her dignity there was jauntiness, merriment on her thin lips. Though old, she was full of gay anticipation, for she loved to be with her son and to make new friends, as she was always confident of doing" (53). Mrs. Tumulty is described as a very enthusiastic, fun-loving old lady whose interests range from butterfly collecting and bird-watching, to travel books and cowboy stories. She also shows inquisitiveness and a great taste for disasters: "Calamity Mrs. Tumulty relished. Disaster opened her heart" (56). She enjoys herself a great deal at Rose's house, mostly by interfering in other people's business, yet she feigns deep indignation when she becomes aware that she has been used by her son as a pretext to be close to Emily.

The vividness with which Isabella, Rose, and Mrs. Tumulty are described greatly enlivens what would otherwise be a rather weak novel. The novel's main fault may be its lack of unity: next to her main plot, Taylor sketches a number of secondary intrigues which could firmly support her story. Yet, as she chooses not to pursue these fertile topics, the story appears incomplete. The novel, which does not illustrate Taylor's dominant theme of failed relationships and loneliness, appears derivative in content.

Chapter Five

Portrait of a Period

A Game of Hide and Seek (1951) and *In a Summer Season* (1961) both show the awakening of a keener social awareness in Taylor's fiction. In both novels, Taylor describes characters who have infringed upon social rules and who try to accept the subsequent social pressures. The two novels also betray a considerable nostalgia for the prewar years, constantly described as a safe and stable era. Finally, if the two novels deal almost exclusively with love, Taylor lays much stress upon the disillusionments which it unfailingly brings. *A Game of Hide and Seek* and *In a Summer Season,* which are among her best-known novels, are dispirited stories in which Taylor's latent pessimism is given full play.

A Game of Hide and Seek

A Game of Hide and Seek is the particularly touching story of a first love which goes wrong. Vesey and Harriet fall in love when they are eighteen but through self-doubt, diffidence, and despair, they fail each other and drift apart. When they meet again twenty years later, they find that, although their love is still intact, it is too late for them; life has inexorably separated them.

The novel is divided into two sections. The first part, which takes place in the early thirties, describes Harriet and Vesey's first awareness of love during a long summer, and the few months of disillusionment following their separation. The second part, which occurs twenty years later, relates Harriet's life as the wife of Charles Jephcott, a wealthy provincial lawyer, and mother of Betsy, a fifteen-year-old schoolgirl. Vesey's sudden reappearance in what seems a well-organized domestic life provokes confusion and disorder. Their few clandestine meetings must end when Harriet's household shows signs of falling apart and when Vesey becomes so ill that he has to be taken home by his mother.

The whole novel betrays a determination to live in the past and expresses considerable nostalgia for the bygone days of innocence. Most of the characters in the novel long for their youth; and, in the case of Harriet and Vesey, the regrets are acute. There is, in *A Game of Hide and Seek,* a subtle glorification of youth seen as a time of unlimited opportunities. As the title of the novel indicates, Taylor also implies that one's youth pre-determines the rest of one's life. The games of hide and seek which Harriet and Vesey used to play with their younger cousins have repercussions on the rest of their lives. Throughout their adulthood, Harriet and Vesey keep hiding and seeking their love for each other. The novel also focuses on the early thirties, a time of certainty, confidence, and happiness. By comparison, the fifties stand for total confusion, uncertainty, and chaos. Marriages break up; families fall apart; the old order has been destroyed.

The first section of the novel contrasts markedly with the rest of the book. Reminiscent of Virginia Woolf, both in tone and technique, the descriptions of first love show Taylor resorting to impressionistic devices; she selects a few special moments of awareness during which Harriet and Vesey discover each other, then she hastens, almost feverishly, over the rest of the narrative. This particular device intensifies the feeling of nostalgia for this special time which, even as it is being related, already seems part of the past.

Throughout their middle age, Harriet and Vesey mourn the days of their carefree youth. The summers were long, the weather was clement. " 'How different when we were young,' Vesey said. 'We never had weather like this. . . .' "[1] Choked with regrets, they have forgotten the awkwardness and heart-aches they experienced then; they are unaware that the youth they are hankering for was their chief handicap, that middle age and its commitments is also the time of self-awareness and revelations. Yet Taylor's evocation of the bygone days is quite compelling largely because the two characters understand them-selves now. " 'When we were young,' Vesey said, 'I never did know what you were thinking. I had the burden of taking all the risks, initiating everything' " (240).

Taylor establishes an interesting parallel between Harriet and Vesey's youth and their middle age. Their youth is bathed in sunlight, their middle age in fog, rain, and mist: "Outside, the fog was a smoke breathed out by some foul mouth. Obscurely, it enfolded them. It *was* a night to have chosen, they said: part of their general helplessness" (235). Yet, in the summer of their youth, neither Vesey nor Harriet had the power to relate to one another. Too often, they were at odds: "All through the long winter and the spring, she would not have him near her; yet, now, standing so close beside him, the moment which should have been so precious was worse than useless: it shrank, and stopped and curdled" (44).

Through Harriet's mother, Lillian, and Vesey's Aunt Caroline, Taylor evokes the particular nostalgia which the two ex-suffragettes feel for their days of struggle. Both miss the solidarity and the sense of purpose which they once felt. They have nothing to fight for now and, as a result, seem to have lost their sense of identity. Harriet feels oppressed by her mother's ideals and high expectations of her. She also senses, with a sense of alienation, that her mother's proudest moment in life was her brief stay in prison. When Lillian feels at a loss socially, she cannot help mentioning it "to support herself, to keep in touch with her own world, which had seemed eclipsed" (64). Taylor displays an amused contempt for the foibles of the two aging feminists who cling to their eventful past, yet she also draws an interesting parallel between Lillian's generation and her daughter's. Unambiguously, Taylor points out that the younger generation's lack of ideals and moral strength can only result in a number of wasted lives.

A Game of Hide and Seek is a pessimistic novel which explores Taylor's growing concern for wasted existences. Relentlessly, Taylor describes how human beings fail themselves and others through a series of wrong choices. It is a dispiriting notion, one that Taylor will explore again in her later novels.

In her very rich and complex portrait of Vesey MacMillan, Taylor has created a memorable character—undeniably the center and the key to the novel—but also the very essence of a wasted man. In the first part of the novel, Vesey is portrayed as a troubled, unstable adolescent who craves for approval and acceptance. Taylor implies that the source of Vesey's emotional

instability lies in his dubious background: a stern uncompromising father who has always ignored him, and a flighty self-absorbed mother who "treated him, at best, with an amused
kindliness" (30). His mother views him as "a beloved marmoset
on a chain" and uses him to show herself off. In this unfavorable
atmosphere, Vesey has had little opportunity to mature emotionally. Moreover, he soon develops the paranoid feeling of being
singled out, of being constantly watched. At school, loneliness
and pride make him appear aloof and condescending; soon,
feeling rejected by others, he develops a streak of cruelty from
which no one is safe. Harriet later tells him: "When you are
hurt, you lay waste all around you" (44). Vesey's feelings for
Harriet spring for his desperate need for her uncritical acceptance of him. "Indeed it had begun to seem to him that only
she was set against the great weight of disapproval he felt upon
him" (30).

The tragedy of Vesey's existence resides in the fact that, even
though he is presented as bright and talented, his early inability
to "connect" makes an outcast of him. As a sense of failure
weighs on every attempt he makes to give a purpose to his
life, he soon turns to self-destruction. He longs to tell Harriet:
"I can only fail. Never expect anything. Because of some flaw
in me, some wrongness, I can neither succeed nor admit defeat
and between the two wait cynically for nothing whatsoever.
When I am touched, I give a false note, like a cracked glass's.
A note of cruelty, or scorn" (104).

Taylor contrasts Vesey's personality with Charles Jephcott's.
Charles, the son of an eccentric actress, was brought up under
similar circumstances to Vesey's, yet managed to overcome those
early handicaps and become a successful lawyer. Vesey, on the
other hand, lacks Charles's basic solidity. Taylor introduces the
notion of a human being's fundamental flaw to explain Vesey's
inability to achieve any sense of personal worth. Presented as
psychologically and emotionally maimed, Vesey can be nothing
but a drifter. He leaves Oxford after only one term to become
an actor. His talent being limited, he never gets past the small
repertory company which was to be his stepping stone. He also
allows his health to deteriorate until he can no longer fend
for himself.

From the beginning of the novel, Taylor impresses a feeling

of doom on the reader. She sets out to show how people can ruin their lives through a series of wrong choices. Young Harriet and Vesey are plagued by the confusions of "shyness, pride, self-consciousness, fear of rebuff or misunderstanding" (4). Moreover, Vesey's cynicism prevents him from indulging in sentimentality which he sees as a weakness. Therefore, he ruthlessly leaves Harriet without a word and later fails to communicate with her. Out of despair, young Harriet makes the fatal mistake of rushing into marriage to a man she does not love. When they meet again twenty years later, Harriet knows that they had their chance and missed it. Besides, she is now trapped by the conventions of provincial middle-class life and by a vague feeling of loyalty to her husband and daughter. She nevertheless hovers uncertainly between her compelling desire to see Vesey and her fear of upsetting her well-organized life. Her inability to make a choice leads her to continue to see Vesey while shrinking away from adultery and lamenting the fact that "The course of unlawful love never does run smooth; or with dignity; or with romance" (250). When she and Vesey go away for a weekend, she finally realizes that the choices have been made.

"If only we were young again!" she said in a tired voice. "And might have a second chance."
"I think perhaps this is supposed to be it," he said doubtfully.
"There aren't second chances; except by ruining other people. . . ." (297)

A critic writes that "it is the nature of their passion to be thwarted."[2] The obstacles to their love stem from their personalities rather than from alienating circumstances. The wrong choices were made long ago. Vesey takes the blame upon himself: "He seemed to have wasted their lives" (284). Yet, from Taylor's point of view, they both wasted their own lives through an inherent flaw in their makeup linked to their emotionally crippled youth. The game of hide and seek is doomed to failure; wrong turns have kept the players from their final union.

If *A Game of Hide and Seek* deals with love, it treats the topic with considerable disillusionment, in a manner reminiscent of Elizabeth Bowen's. The description of love, mostly from Harriet's point of view, is quite compelling in its early stages and unstained by experience. Harriet's feelings for Vesey are stronger than his feelings for her. As she too has suffered the pain of isolation as a child, unable to relate to her slightly exalted mother and feeling constantly inadequate, she sees Vesey as a kindred spirit and develops a lifelong devotion to him. Yet, her happiness with him soon turns into heartaches and bitterness—and this may be where Taylor's pessimism is the most apparent—for they cannot be happy together. Vesey's cynicism behind which he hides his vulnerability is the first jarring note. His callousness dismays Harriet who has to adjust to the idea of loving someone imperfect. Her disillusionment soon becomes perceptible: "Prove to me, she willed him, that love is not what other people describe . . . a trap, an antagonism; or, as it is under this roof, a dull habit" (105). Following the death of her mother, which leaves her alone in the world, Harriet starts to rely more and more on Charles; yet she hardly dares to hope that "for everybody there is perhaps another person who will not fade on approach" (125).

In the second phase of Harriet and Vesey's relationship, Taylor conveys an impression of deeper despair. She hints at intervening years of constant misery "seeing one face constantly in crowds." Charles has become obsessed with Vesey whom he sees, even in his absence, as a permanent threat: "For it was Vesey who had undermined their life together; the idea of him in both their heads" (181–82). When they meet again, even if Harriet and Vesey are closer than they have ever been, they still cannot "connect." Their failure to relate to one another causes them great pain. Taylor depicts a dejected vision of love, for she implies that, despite their deep feelings for each other, her lovers cannot find each other and constantly feel cheated and betrayed.

A Game of Hide and Seek is characterized by a stark realism used by Taylor to emphasize the disillusionment that her characters experience both in their daily lives and in their relationships with one another. Taylor establishes a striking parallel between Harriet and Vesey's ways of living. The beautiful red and white room in Harriet's pretty home contrasts rather grimly with Vesey's sordid lodgings.

The window is over a yard with dust-bins and ferns, and by the window there is a marble-topped washstand that I use for a desk—

very cold to the wrists. The bath has a green stain running down under the geyser and . . . am I depressing you? It's rather like George Gissing perhaps . . . I eat my meals at the washstand, too, and rather nasty they are, and I wrote those letters to you sitting there. Your letters I keep wrapped up in a paper bag in the top right-hand drawer of the chest. I thought you would like to know. My books are in cardboard boxes underneath the bed. (239)

Taylor describes gloomy surroundings to underline the hopelessness of her characters' love for each other. Their brief visit to a small tea shop in London leads to one of her most famous descriptions. "They came to a small tea-shop in a mean street. In the furred darkness it was a dim oasis. A card saying OPEN hung crookedly against the door, and in the window a plate of cakes lay in a strange light, like fossilized cakes in a museum. They looked so permanent. They could no more moulder away, they felt, than could shells or pieces of stone" (236–37). The scene in the tea room during which her characters playfully order the dreadful cakes has a particularly daunting quality. Taylor implies that Harriet and Vesey are toying with reality. Harriet feels a strange dichotomy which allows her to escape mentally. Later, in a final confrontation, she has to face the truth. The hotel to which Vesey and she flee for a weekend proves to be squalid. Her sensitivity is adversely affected by the uncongenial atmosphere.

At the sight of the room, Harriet felt a dismay so private, so profound that she could scarcely breathe: it was a fit culmination to such a journey; a destiny, as well as a destination.
An ancient gas-fire stood in front of a coal-grate, without concealing the litter of matchsticks and cigarette ends behind. She found a shilling for the slot and put a match between the broken ribs, but she felt that for all the blue, roaring light that shot upwards the room would never warm. (293–94)

Taylor conveys the ambiguous notion that Harriet's love for Vesey is severely checked by the grim circumstances which she must endure when she leaves the right path. Taylor also implies that more congenial surroundings might well lessen Harriet's resistance and weaken her resolution to go back to her husband. In the absence of a deep moral sense, Taylor's streak of realism sharply underlines the unrealistic aspects of Harriet and Vesey's hypothetical union.

If no strong moral sense pervades the pages of *A Game of Hide and Seek,* there is, however, a deep belief in the existence of a social order imminent to anyone's passions. Taylor lays much stress upon the importance of marriage as a unit to uphold society: "When she married Charles, she had seemed to wed also a social order. A convert to it, and to provincial life, and keeping house, she had pursued it fanatically and as if she feared censure" (269). Harriet does not allow Vesey to question the institution of marriage. She instinctively feels that, in the changing fifties, she has the moral duty to fight for a rest of stability: "Marriage is an institution. One fails it again and again, but I expect one mustn't begin to question it, or the world falls to pieces . . ." (262).

Taylor also emphasizes the notion of solidarity between human beings within the social framework, indicating clearly that one person's mistakes may bring about the downfall of many others. This burden of responsibility—however purely social—weighs heavily upon Harriet: " 'It is true,' she reflected, 'that we are all members one of another. When one man falls, he takes others down in his arms' " (288). Harriet therefore views her responsibilities more as an exterior display of goodwill than as a deeply felt duty of love. Feeling like a modern Madame Bovary, aware of averted glances and whisperings, she feels burdened by her guilt toward society: "Certain that she wreaked ill on all who came near her, and would ruin her husband and her child, she seemed to herself to infect, to contaminate society, whose rules she had never before been tempted to break; which, with the extra spur of her natural inadequacy, she had, in fact, strengthened and maintained" (268–69).

Taylor shows how the smooth surface of Harriet's social life cannot resist the sudden reappearance of Vesey. Her home life becomes a turmoil of misunderstandings and suspicions. Her husband Charles, who is plagued by a deep fear of rejection and latent insecurity, immediately feels threatened. His perceptiveness allows him to detect her lies and small deceptions and he suffers great jealousy. Their daughter Betsy, fascinated by Vesey, starts imagining that he is her real father. As a result her life becomes chaos, she becomes moody and unpredictable, and her grades at school deteriorate.

Taylor clearly conveys the obvious paradox of Harriet's life.

In spite of her constant desire to obey social rules, Harriet is shown as failing as both a wife and a mother. Her marriage to Charles, which started as an act of desperation, has not turned out very well, in spite of the convincing facade which she presents to the world. Charles remains the stranger whom she married twenty years ago. " 'Marriage does not solve mysteries,' she thought. 'It creates and deepens them' " (148). When Charles is left on the edge of ruin by an unscrupulous associate, Harriet bravely rallies around. As the novel ends, however, there is little hope left for a deeper relationship. Harriet vows to make a new start but Taylor's familiar, ambiguous note is present: " 'I will be different . . . You shall never be worried again. . . . If you could forgive me. . . .' She made a fence of little phrases, which seemed a treachery to herself" (306).

The novel's dismal ending seems to stress Taylor's pessimistic trend. Vesey finally makes one selfless gesture. By telling Harriet that he is being sent to South Africa by his father, he breaks all connections between them. When Harriet comes to say good-bye, however, the very sick Vesey is being fetched by his mother. Through a mist he barely sees Harriet's face, yet his last vision of her bears a symbolical significance for it recalls their youth: "She put her bunch of flowers down on a chair and said his name and took him in her arms" (313). Taylor hints that Vesey may never recover. The separation between the two lovers is to be total.

Despite the grim ending, fleetingly, throughout the novel, there remains the conviction that "life is short and happiness a good thing, to be made much of" (243). *A Game of Hide and Seek* is an extremely striking novel that offers a sad—but never bitter—vision of love. The game of hide and seek, which Taylor's two lovers have consistently been playing, has allowed them a few moments of happiness and Taylor implies—in what may be her more optimistic outlook—that despite the pain love makes life worth living. This last conviction attenuates the deeply felt despondency of the novel.

In a Summer Season

In a Summer Season takes place in the beautiful Thames Valley within sight of Windsor castle; in fact, the characters turn to face the castle in times of stress, as if the symbol of the Establishment could give them the reassurance they are all seeking. The large house in which Kate and her family live, an early Victorian converted vicarage, has all the characteristics of gracious upper-middle-class living. It is located within commuting distance of London, and Kate lives among her friends who own similarly large houses, "gardens full of flowering trees, bright gravel drives, and tennis courts."[3]

The large comfortable home houses a strange conglomeration of people. With Kate, who is in her forties, and her new husband Dermot, ten years her junior, live Kate's two children, twenty-two-year-old Tom and fifteen-year-old Louisa. The household also includes Kate's Aunt Ethel, a lively spinster who plays the cello, and the well-traveled cook, Mrs. Meacock, who, in her spare time, is also compiling an anthology called "Five Thousand and One Witty Sayings."

It is the life of a wealthy society which Taylor describes in her novel. Having been left a substantial amount of money by her first husband, Kate is a woman of independent means on which she wisely keeps sole control. Her new husband Dermot has never held a job in his life. He is content to go to races and to drink in pubs with Kate, who, too often, is aware that they are wasting their lives: "We're all of us just passing time. . . . A lack of purpose was an infection Dermot may have given them" (149). Against this background of money and idleness, Taylor is quick to outline the gradual loss of self-respect which Dermot experiences.

Set during a summer described as "the best summer in two hundred years," the novel is bathed in a golden light. Even though Taylor intersperses her story with nostalgic references to previous summers and lost friendships, it seems that, despite the unsettled mood, nothing tragic could take place during such a privileged summer. Taylor, however, sets out to prove the opposite and the glorious summer, which is to end tragically, witnesses the slow disintegration of Kate and Dermot's unlikely marriage.

In a Summer Season shows how much Taylor relies on love and its complications as a theme. The novel deals with different kinds of love. Taylor establishes a stark contrast between Kate's two marriages. Her first marriage to a man with whom she had many affinities, shared the same tastes and sense of values, had brought out the best in her. Feeling on safe ground, she had always been a good wife and an attentive mother. Looking back, Kate realizes that the past provided a sense of safety that the shifting present denies her: "We believed that we were safe, that our love, so long as it lasted—and we were certain it would last till death—was its own, and our, safeguard. We were the lucky ones" (88). Her marriage to Alan was the union of two minds, evenings spent at home listening to Beethoven quartets or reading Henry James; she felt restless at times. Now the roles are reversed. Her second husband is an attractive younger man, a charming drifter, with whom she has very little in common. Their relationship is essentially physical. Her Aunt Ethel provides a cynical analysis of the marriage: "Without being too brutal, one must admit that she has bought him for herself with the money Alan left her, and one day he, Dermot, will begin to find that being her property is irksome. Then, when the physical side grows less important, she may think she hasn't got her money's worth" (45). What Ethel does not take into consideration, however, is the fact that Dermot loves Kate deeply and finds much self-esteem in doing so: "His love for her was his chief pride" (28).

Presented as a parasite full of unlikely schemes, Dermot, who is now trying to grow mushrooms in an outhouse, seems to turn into failure everything he attempts.

She was still often surprised by what Dermot did not know, and it was a puzzle to her that he could have spent so many years at school and have so little to show for them. His handwriting was childish, his spelling eccentric, and when he played darts he could seldom subtract his score. All of his modest efforts to make money ended in confusions of figures from which he could only extricate the fact that he had less than he had had when he started. The mushroom-growing would be the same, in spite of all the people he had heard about who had made so much money from similar schemes. (43)

Dermot's lack of purpose seems to have contaminated the whole household. Kate, in particular, worries constantly about the negative influence that Dermot has over her son Tom who, to everyone's surprise, has become extremely fond of his stepfather: "Allies at race-meetings, leaning over bars, laughing at their betters, as they called it, they seemed, but for the worship on one side, much the same age" (24). Dermot's slack habits, his heavy drinking, and the fact that he constantly encourages Tom to rebel worry Kate greatly, especially when Tom jokingly points out to her: "Your new husband is a bad example to us young lads" (24).

As Kate's young husband, Dermot is constantly made to feel inadequate and uncertain how to behave. His total lack of self-restraint follows a well-established pattern: "His drinking evenings had the same pattern always, as she knew. Caution, exhilaration, aggressiveness, were followed by the diminuendo of face-saving, self-reproach, reproach, attempts at recovery, back to caution again" (35).

Taylor is intent to prove how infringing upon a social rule can alter the life of a woman. Being married to a man ten years her junior is a strain with which Kate has difficulty coping. Having anticipated the problems likely to arise from such a union, Kate nevertheless struggles to solve them. Taylor describes two interludes at Kate's hairdresser which underlines the increasing uncertainty and self-doubts experienced by her heroine. As she has difficulty accepting her new identity as Dermot's wife, her uneasiness induces her to make gradual changes in her hair style. Kate has also become vague, disorganized, at a loss—traits that reflect "the general demoralization" brought about by her second marriage: "Everything was too much for her, whether getting up for breakfast or seeing that Tom behaved himself" (45). The lack of constancy which characterizes Kate's recent behavior deeply disturbs her daughter Louisa who wonders why her mother has changed so drastically. The totality of Kate's energy is clearly used up by her relationship with Dermot whom she loves despite their many incompatibilities. She constantly tries to conciliate him, using all the tact she can muster not to hurt his susceptibilities, for Dermot's lack of self-esteem is a festering wound: "As soon as she was alone with Dermot after dinner Kate realized how cleverly she must put her sentences together; tactful phrases must seem careless, but the carelessness must not verge on indifference or she would be accused of condescending" (26).

In a manner reminiscent of Austen's, Taylor describes various examples of unsettled love. Noting that "The love there was in the house seemed fitful, leaving uneasiness" (105), Taylor describes, at some length, the feelings that Kate's son, Tom, soon experiences for beautiful Araminta Thornton, a childhood friend, whom he had not seen for a number of months. A bewildering creature who fascinates all the men she meets, Araminta is a strange mixture of childish bad behavior and cool sophistication. She also appears as slippery as an eel when Tom tries to catch her. Her coolness and detachment, amounting to indifference, constantly mystify him. Tom views her developing friendship with Dermot with hostility and jealousy. He is not aware that Araminta and Dermot are two of a kind: both are self-absorbed, lazy hedonists. Her accidental death in Dermot's new car shatters him totally, and Taylor hints that, despite his youth, Tom is suffering from a deeper shock than his mother from Dermot's death.

Taylor depicts yet a different kind of love, a form of selfless, simple devotion which Louisa, at fifteen, feels for the young curate Father Blizzard. Taylor's description of this first love is both touching and amusing. As Louisa experiences difficulties adjusting to the changes brought about by her mother's second marriage, she feels the need to confide in Father Blizzard and feels greatly uplifted by his sympathy. The relationship ends when Louisa returns to school and when the curate who has run into a theological controversy with his vicar has to leave the village. His gift to Louisa of a gold bracelet makes her totally happy as only—Taylor implies—the very young can be. Taylor deals with Louisa with amused sympathy: "Goodness gracious, he patted her head. Should she be walking out with him like this? Oh, dear, she ought to know better than to stand there staring after him. . . . That's right, dear girl, you come along in. He must have looked back. She's waving" (66).

In spite of all the conflicts and pain of unsettled love, *In a Summer Season* is not a gloomy book. Taylor excels at describing the social interplay in which her characters are involved in their daily lives. A critic notes: "Mrs. Taylor's completely absorbing and very fine novel is bound, as a matter of fact, to recall Jane Austen on almost every page in spite of its modern trappings of motorcars, cocktail parties and cosmetics."[4] Taylor occasionally indulges in a social irony reminiscent of Austen. Society

also plays a dramatic role in the novel which reminds the reader
of a play. Kate and Dermot's relationship is under observation
from different quarters, which allows Taylor to give various
insights on their marital strife. Dermot knows he is being
watched and he behaves unnaturally as a result. Ethel's critical—
yet not unkind—scrutiny provides a constant analysis of the
situation. Mrs. Meacock, the temperamental cook, also expects
signs of downfall: "He's not himself, thought Mrs. Meacock,
for under that roof, and elsewhere too, they were watching
for the marriage to disintegrate. Conscious of this, Dermot became self-conscious" (63). Despite her young age, Louisa offers
a surprisingly acute insight in her mother's erratic behavior.
"And now she's so different, such a very different person, much
too gay for her age one minute, and over-tired and irritable
the next; drinks too much, I should think, can't be bothered
with her old friends—and after all, they're *my* friends' parents,
most of them, and I've got to live in the place" (59).

The watchful audience, "the chorus waiting to comment on
and explain their downfall" (110), puts enormous strain on
the relationship for both Kate and Dermot know that they do
not conform to society's rules. To escape from the constant
attention, they go away to the Cotswolds for a few days, and
are much happier by themselves. Yet, even outside their social
circle, they arouse curiosity and speculations: "A strangely
matched pair, it was thought. The difference in their ages puzzled
the country people, who were convinced—by their too positive
happiness—of something illicit between them" (109–10).

Taylor tends to lay much emphasis on what she sees as the
generation gap between Kate and Dermot. Clear-minded Kate
is aware that "There were three distinct generations in the house:
her Aunt Ethel's, then her own, and her children's. Between
her's and Tom's and Lou's, on the mezzanine floor, as it were,
was Dermot's" (23). It is clear, nevertheless, that Dermot's
immaturity makes the ten years' difference seem more important.
In outlook and mentality, he is much closer to Tom, which
prompts Louisa to comment: "Blood isn't really thicker than
water. Don't you think Tom is much more like Dermot than
our own father?" (40). The gap between Kate and Dermot
becomes acute when Dermot meets the Thorntons for the first
time. Whereas it is clear that he finds twenty-year-old Araminta
extremely attractive, he calls her father, Kate's peer, "A jolly

nice old codger." Nothing could outline more drastically the gulf which separates him from Kate at that stage.

Taylor underlines the increasing uneasiness which Kate feels in her ill-matched marriage. Her efforts to behave normally on social occasions seem doomed to failure. Feeling that he constantly fails here, Dermot indulges in both self-punishment and antagonism. The social drama is painful to Kate who feels that society will eventually defeat them. "Nothing happened, she was thinking. Nothing was said. But one day, in this or other country, it will be said. It was a great relief to be spared it for the present. She felt drained of strength and patience and was suffering the boredom for which she would later be blamed" (31).

The return of the Thorntons provides the additional impetus that brings the novel to its climax. Whereas Charles Thornton implicitly challenges Dermot's precarious position as Kate's husband, his daughter Araminta appears as a very subtle threat to Kate. Taylor uses light social comedy to bring out the increasing uneasiness and tension. Charles Thornton immediately tries to "place" Dermot, to the latter's great disquiet. "They were walking in circles round each other, Kate thought—both Dermot and Charles. When she had introduced them, Dermot had shaken hands with an air of boyish respect, almost adding 'sir' to his greeting, and Charles seemed to try to avoid looking at him or to show more than ordinary interest" (130). Mistakenly assuming that Dermot shares his wife's enthusiasm for Henry James, Charles refers to a friend as Mrs. Gereth, thus confusing Dermot who replies: "I've never met Mrs. Gereth" (134). Deeply embarrassed, Kate recalls having once exclaimed: "I could never have married a man who did not simply dote on Jane Austen and Henry James" (134). Furthermore, the "appreciation of music" evening instigated by Charles also shows Dermot as a philistine. By describing the scene from his point of view, however, Taylor conveys much sympathy for his plight. After observing Kate's expression and deciding that music does not suit her, Dermot wonders—in a manner strangely similar to that of Amis's Jim Dixon—if he might weep with boredom or go simply mad:

Cymbals clashed, and he started violently. They were working themselves into a frenzy. Surely—he dared hope—they could not sustain such a fury of sound much longer. The climax was such a wonderful relief, and in happy gratitude he was just about to jump up and fill glasses when a single flute meandered into a solo passage; dying away, but not quite; returning with more assurance and inviting—Dermot was in no doubt—the whole orchestra to keep it company, which, one instrument after another, it did. (173)

The social irony lightens the mood, yet Taylor allows strong undercurrents to be perceptible. Her social comedy lays bare the vulnerabilities and weaknesses of her characters and, by subtly exacerbating their passions, makes a tragic ending seem unavoidable.

In a Summer Season is another novel in which Taylor indulges in what may be described as a melodramatic trend. Her eighth novel displays a different pattern from her earlier ones for Taylor discards her usually ambiguous ending, much like leaving off in mid-sentence, to close her novel on a final note, allowing no doubt in the reader's mind as to the fate of its characters. The accidental death in a car accident of Dermot and Araminta seems a fit culmination to the social drama which has been enacted in the novel. It has not been in Taylor's habit to introduce violent disasters in her quiet, well-bred comedy of social intercourse. Yet the exacerbated passions and strong emotions lead, with an implacable logic, to a violent climax. To placate restless Dermot, Kate has agreed to trade in the old family car for a new faster model. A heavy drinker, Dermot often drives the car under the influence of alcohol. Both he and Araminta are said to love speed and share a certain recklessness. Tired of being constantly challenged by his precarious situation, Dermot also finds reassurance with a younger undemanding woman who accepts him as he is.

Even though *In a Summer Season* is not a gloomy novel, Taylor hints, from the beginning, that Kate and Dermot's marriage is ill-fated. The fact that everyone expects the marriage to disintegrate is a guarantee of downfall for the unlucky couple, for society traditionally upholds marriages, and the strain of its disapproval seriously compromises the chances of success of any marriage. Before the return of the Thorntons, Kate feels a sense of doom. Perceptive Louisa also has premonitions of disasters becoming aware that "something was being set in train which she could not follow" (129). The exasperation Tom feels for the calculated coldness of beautiful Araminta slowly builds up and causes him to feel intensely destructive: "He was reminded of the exasperation he had suffered as a child when a balloon had floated away from his grasp. He would reach it, but as soon as his fingers touched it, it would bob on ahead of him, until, broken with fury, he had screamed and thrown a stone at it. If he couldn't have it, he would rather it were destroyed. But I don't want Minty hurt, he thought" (205). The afterthought does little to dispel the impression made by the prophetic wish.

Critics have called *In a Summer Season* a "tea-table' tragedy"[5] or have argued that "the depths which the story plumbs are only those of a pool made in a shallow hollow by a gentle spring rain."[6] There is a fundamental lightness of tone in the novel that may be thought to belie the tragedy about to occur. Taylor uses the means of social comedy to delve into the tragic consequences of transgressing on social rules. Yet she never becomes oppressive, and her quietness of tone often causes her to be underestimated. She is far from being a weak writer, however, for, in the true tradition of Jane Austen, her social comedy probes the depths of the human heart.

Chapter Six

Romance and Realism

The Soul of Kindness, published in 1964, and *The Wedding Group,* published in 1968, mark the apex of Taylor's career as a novelist. Both novels display, to a full extent, all the elements that have won Taylor so much critical acclaim over the years. In these two fine psychological studies, Taylor demonstrates her talent for understatement and economy of means, along with her well-known quietness of tone. More importantly, in these two novels which establish her as a mature writer, Taylor begins to reconcile the old tradition of Jane Austen with the new realistic trend of the contemporary novel. In both novels, she establishes a parallel between romance, the nostalgia for the old world, and realism, the acceptance of the new state of affairs produced by the welfare state. Both novels show a positive effort to accept the new order, even if this acceptance generates a certain amount of despondency and despair which are more perceptible in these two novels than in any earlier ones.

The Soul of Kindness

Elizabeth Taylor dedicated her ninth novel to Elizabeth Bowen Cameron, thus acknowledging a link that has often been noted by critics. The resemblance, however, is one of spirit rather than one of style. Both novelists write in the domestic tradition of Jane Austen, dealing with a limited social field and permeating their novels with nostalgia. Both show delicacy, finesse, and restraint. While Bowen's novels deal with disillusionment and the loss of innocence, Taylor's novels deal with the lack of communication between human beings and the resulting isolation. Taylor, who has been called "the modern man's Jane Austen," may be closer to Austen than Bowen is, for her novels are suffused with humor and a gentle irony that sets her apart from Bowen.

The Soul of Kindness may be Taylor's most representative novel since it embodies all the characteristics that have made her reputation as a novelist. Particularly striking in its nostalgic description of middle-class life and values, the novel centers on the meek yet devastating portrait of Flora, the "soul of kindness," and on the theme of failed relationships and loneliness. A subtlety of composition is indeed this novel's hallmark.

The Soul of Kindness deals with the genteel life of middle-class people who, in the drab conditions of postwar Britain, have managed to retain a reasonably high standard of living. The story takes place in the Thames Valley, a high spot of upper-middle-class living, and in London's St. John's Wood, a conservatively fashionable part of London. There is nothing drab about the way either Mrs. Secretan or her daughter Flora Quartermaine live. Both own large houses run by housekeepers and enjoy the luxuries provided by a substantial income. The only intimation to hardship is the description of Flora's husband's sufferings as he democratically braves the rush hour in the London underground every night.

From the beginning of the story, Taylor makes it clear that she is dealing with a privileged class. The novel's opening scene is a wedding in the Thames Valley, the bride surrounded by doves, while her guests drink champagne in the marquee. While Taylor paints quite a convincing picture of middle-class life throughout the novel, there remains a definite sense of nostalgia as if what she described belonged to a remote past. Flora's evocation of her youth conjures up revealing reactions from one of her friends: "A *toile de Jouy* world of innocent country pleasures, he said to himself, almost moving his lips as he paced about the room, and could imagine the girls dressed as shepherdesses, one pushing a swing, the other flying upwards, ribbons fluttering. A quite different world from any nowadays, with different weather."[1] The unreality of the scene, which Taylor is quick to convey, bespeaks the changes that have since occurred. Through old-fashioned Mrs. Secretan, Taylor deplores the new state of affairs produced by the welfare state:

Everything around her was changing for the worst, not only the polluted Thames but the ugly cement lamp standards that had replaced the Victorian ones in the village street, the new brash supermarket, the council houses beyond the church, and the block of flats where once her old friend, Lady Brotherhood, had her villa. It was a village no longer, it was an overcrowded, noisy suburb. People had to live somewhere. Whenever she grumbled about the state of affairs, she always added that, grudgingly. But why here? Why did they not go up to Scotland, where she understood cottages were empty and derelict. (141–42)

There is a touch of social complacency in Mrs. Secretan, as in most of Taylor's characters. Richard Quartermaine feels truly outraged as he has to endure the indignities of rush-hour traveling in the London underground: "Rush-hour tedium, hanging about in uncongenial places such as this one, threatened his reason, he thought, filling the vacuum of his mind with nonsensical names, printing banal pictures on his retina" (18). Richard, however, is in a different position from Mrs. Secretan. He has not always belonged to the wealthy minority which is Mrs. Secretan's natural element, and this knowledge makes him self-conscious at times: "He envied those like his mother-in-law. They were so comfortable that it was hardly fair—wonderful to be so serene, to have cupboards empty of skeletons, to take all privileges for granted—education, leisure (the Miss Folleys, Mrs. Lodges who made it possible). The security of 'birth' seemed to him a chancy thing" (102). Richard is not a true declassé for his father's early affluence allowed him to send his son to a public school, but he has kept the stigmas of his class; this is an interesting notion that Taylor unfortunately does not develop.

Elizabeth Taylor, who has always been thought of as an underrated novelist, largely because of her quietness and her restraint, achieves a great success with her gentle yet devastating portrait of beautiful Flora Quartermaine, model daughter, wife, and friend. Taylor's economy of means is more effective than strident and forceful denunciations could ever be. Her heroine is described as blonde, tall, and beautiful. Born in a wealthy family, she has been raised in the pleasant and peaceful Thames Valley by a protective mother whose sole purpose in life must have been to shield her daughter from the ugliness of reality. Flora, who grew up in a vacuum, remained innocent and trusting but also immature and thoughtless.

Owing her well-chosen name to the goddess of flowers, Flora
has been worshipped from birth. At school, her friend Meg
Driscoll took over Mrs. Secretan's role, "for it was clear from
the day that Flora arrived there that what Mrs. Secretan had
done—the cherishing, the protecting—could not be lightly broken off" (8). When Flora gets married, this responsibility falls
to her husband, Richard, and her housekeeper, Mrs. Lodge.

Even though Flora is constantly described as "as good as
gold," there is little evidence to support the notion. She is presented as meek and mild, always telling her friends exactly what
they want to hear. As she basks in others' admiration and love,
she strives never to aggrieve or antagonize them. Convinced
that she has everything that one could wish, Flora feels complacent toward her luckless friends and tries, in her own way, to
make them happy.

Flora's innocence, upon which much stress is laid, has been
fostered at great pains by those around her. Her mother and
husband, in particular, have set themselves the exhausting task
of keeping it intact: "But we've preserved the face pretty well,
between us, Richard thought, fearing not ageing lines but the
loss of innocence. So far, and by the skin of his teeth, he felt.
The face was his responsibility now, and it would surely be
his fault if it were altered, if the Boticelli calm were broken,
or the appealing gaze veiled" (76). Both characters are constantly filled with the fear of failing Flora, of not being up to
her high standards, of letting harsh reality intrude upon her
dreamworld. When Mrs. Secretan suspects that she is seriously
ill, she tries to keep the worries from Flora, totally unaware
that, by taking Richard into her confidence, she causes a marital
rift. She insists on protecting her daughter from the grim reality
of death: "When it came, she had resolved to be as peaceful
as she could. It would be the last thing she could do for Flora—
to take perhaps the ugly fear of death out of her life" (196).

Taylor manages to turn Flora's innocence into a totally alienating trait. Besides being an unconscious means of putting pressure
upon others, it seems little more than bland naiveté. Little by
little, Taylor adds other touches. The reader soon becomes
aware—probably more acutely than Taylor had intended—that
Flora is a deeply self-centered character. The fact that she is
totally unaware of it makes her all the more harmful. It seems

normal to her that others should gravitate around her and orga-
nize their lives to make her happy. Her "kindness" consists
largely in helping her friends for self-gratification. Unfortunately, Flora knows nothing about people. Her understanding
of their lives is so limited that any interference on her part is
bound to cause havoc. Ironically, she spends most of her time
worrying about her friends' misfortunes and making what Taylor
slyly calls "inconvenient plans for other people's pleasure."

Her first victim is her friend Meg for whom she feels deep
pity: "If she could get Meg settled, Flora had decided, she herself
would be quite happy, but her friend thought that she went
about it in strange ways and wondered what, if anything at
all, Flora knew about people" (37). Flora introduces Meg to
men whom she considers eligible. When Meg falls in love with
one of them, Patrick Barlow, a homosexual writer, her life becomes a misery, much to Flora's chagrin. Flora then accuses
people of being "gossipy and fanciful" about Patrick, and nevertheless tries to coax him into marrying Meg. His subsequent
refusal she interprets as sheer selfishness.

Her next victim is her widowed father-in-law, Percy Quartermaine, who, until then, led a contented life, sharing his time
between his home and the apartment of his mistress. Uncon-
sciously imposing her own values of middle-class respectability
onto the aging couple, Flora starts a campaign to make them
marry. She successfully plays on each party's feelings of responsibility and instills guilt into them. As Flora simply knows that
they will be much happier when they are married, she has no
respite until she achieves her goal: "The real titbit of news
this time—too good to wait until after unpacking—was Flora's
personal triumph: that, through her tireless, but subtle machina-
tions, she had persuaded Ba to be betrothed to Percy and Percy
to imagine that he wanted this" (101). She ignores their subsequent difficulties in adjusting to a change which they had not
wanted in the first place: "The old order had been so much
better—to be alone in the day-time with his piano and his gramo-
phone, to look forward to visiting his mistress in the evenings.
He had no mistress now, and nothing to look forward to, either"
(242).

Her last and most vulnerable victim is Kit Driscoll, Meg's
young brother, who literally worships her. Kit dreams of becom-

ing an actor in spite of a recognized lack of talent. Flora, nevertheless, encourages him constantly: " 'I have faith in him,' said Flora, with what Patrick had once called her Early Christian look. She lifted her chin, and her eyes were steady. She glowed with confidence" (54). In an attempt to behave in a responsible manner, Kit finds himself a job, to Flora's annoyance. When he gets sick and Flora visits him, she perceives his feeling of depression and tries to instill new faith in him: " 'Kit, dear, I truly believe in you.' 'Yes, I think you do. It's that that worries me when I fail' " (225). The novel culminates in Kit's suicide attempt, a harsh condemnation of Flora's constant interference in others' lives. Faced for the first time with the possibility of deserving a blame, Flora goes through a brief but intense crisis. Seeing herself suddenly as "someone she could not bear to live with", she disintegrates until, with the help of her doubtful friends, she reconstructs her self-image of kindness and goodwill.

Taylor's "genteel flaying of Flora Quartermaine,"[3] for all its cleverness and effectiveness, is also ambivalent. Flora is not described as a real human being. Her husband Richard feels constant frustration in spite of the fact that Flora seems a perfect wife and he is totally devoted to her. He suffers from stomach ulcers caused by the constant pressure under which he feels. His wife strikes him as having little grasp on reality. For a while, he seeks the company of another woman, a neighbor, who, at least, is real. Yet his reluctance to get involved in anyone else's life, coupled with his fear of discovering what may prove to be a wasps' nest, prevent him from deepening their friendship. In many ways, Flora is a passive and pale creation who shows few strong feelings or emotions and whose gentleness and meekness appear fairly unpalatable at times. One may wonder how intentional this is on Taylor's part. Her chosen economy of means backfires in the sense that she has created a character who strikes the reader as somewhat bland.

There is a great deal of irony in Flora's situation, for others put her on the pedestal on which she now stands. Her mother, her husband, her friends, all contribute to keep her in a vacuum of complacency and self-satisfaction. Flora has no grasp on reality because she has never been allowed to come into contact with the real world. The lifelong worshipping and constant admiration to which she has been subjected have only cultivated her egotism. She has never been given a chance to mature into a responsible human being. When the opportunity finally arises, her friends deny her the chance, believing, perhaps with justification, that she is not capable of it. They are also choosing the easy way out for their own comfort. As Taylor implies, self-interests prevail in the end.

The Soul of Kindness is a remarkable novel because of the deftness with which Elizabeth Taylor has organized its various elements. Flora holds the center of the stage, and the other characters are shown as gravitating around her. The novel begins in complete harmony; everyone concurs to praise Flora's kindness, her generosity, her thoughtfulness. Then, little by little, increasing dissonance becomes perceptible. Her husband shows frustration, her friends disloyalty and exasperation; her housekeeper wants to leave. Then, when the climax occurs, all hell breaks loose. Lucidity suddenly dawns on a number of people who come to realize that Flora is "as ingenuously destructive as a rabid lamb."[3] They judge her, and condemn her, but pity— the old enemy—is at work again. Flora's ravaged beauty is a spectacle no one wishes to witness: "She's destroying herself before our very eyes. I can't bear destruction" (243). Her friend Meg holds out much longer, being the strongest and the most affected: "It's our punishment for having had that horrid glimpse of her she had herself. She'll go on and on until we rally round and build up the image again" (243). The novel ends in apparent harmony: the characters rally round their goddess, without conviction, but out of a sense of duty. Nothing outwardly has changed.

Critics have praised Taylor's "strategic characterization and fictional grace."[4] Flora is surrounded by a well-chosen cast of characters, all sharply individualized and some delightfully funny. Next to childishly angry Percy Quartermaine, there is wise, worldly Ba, his new Jewish wife. Diligent, industrious Mrs. Secretan, also a constant worrier, lives with the pathologically imaginative Miss Folley. Peaceful, gentle Meg lives with her young brother Kit who is constantly assailed by self-doubts. Patrick Barlow lives alone in his spacious apartment.

Opposite Flora, Taylor has introduced a character whose purpose in the novel is to counterbalance Flora's negative influence.

Liz Corbett, a painter, is Flora's exact opposite. She is unattractive and coarse. Unlike the other characters who bask in Flora's goodwill, Liz, who has never met her, feels strong hostility toward her: "Her antagonism to Flora was simply that the kind of woman she imagined her to be was the kind that she had always scorned. She connected her with romance, charm, fashion, elegance, fine feelings—all spurious things, she considered" (87). Liz's brief, rather sordid affair with Kit contrasts starkly with his long-lasting veneration for Flora. Yet Liz's influence over him is far more beneficial than Flora's could ever be. Baiting him into finding a job and seeing less of Flora, Liz gives Kit's life a new sense of direction.

Taylor deals with Flora and Liz in a paradoxical manner. Whereas coarse Liz creates beauty out of ugliness, order out of chaos, beautiful Flora wreaks havoc wherever she goes. Flora is associated with charm, Liz with crudeness. Flora represents the old order, Liz the new one, with its stridency. Yet, Flora lives in complete self-deception while Liz is outspoken and honest. The paradox goes further. While Taylor describes Flora's kindness to others, she hints that she actually is a destructive creature. While she presents Liz as quite dreadful, Taylor implies that she represents goodness and truth. Readers may, nevertheless, find Flora a more personable character for, and this may be Taylor's ultimate point, are we not all guilty of falling for beauty, charm, and romance?

Taylor has distinguished herself in her character study. "It is a dance of failed relationships," writes Brigid Brophy.[5] As such, *The Soul of Kindness* is one of Taylor's most pessimistic novels. Her portrayal of Meg Driscoll and Patrick Barlow, in particular, is infused with pathos and pity.

Meg Driscoll is presented as the archetypal unlucky girl, with all the troubles in the world: "her mother's death when her brother was still at school, her father's long before, the responsibility of Kit's future, money worries, and a hopeless falling in love—hopeless and impossible to the verge of absurdity, Ba had said" (16). Unlike Flora, Meg has neither beauty nor charm to rely on, yet she has courage and obstinacy, even if she lacks faith in herself or in the future. She struggles along, occasionally indulging in self-pity, watching with fear the years passing by, feeling dowdiness creeping in: "Her life would turn out to be quite different from the one she had dreamed of as a child; it would be like that of Miss Williams at the office, who lived with her invalid mother and never went on a holiday or had an adventure. The books she read were sillier and sillier as the years went by—for reality had become upsetting, the truth disturbing" (80).

With Patrick whom she sees once a week, Meg is happy and wears a look of "gentle radiance." Taylor treats the problem of their relationship with great delicacy and restraint. Even though she hints that theirs are wasted existences, she gives them considerable sympathy.

Like Meg, Patrick is presented as a victim of his own fate. He, too, is hopelessly in love with the wrong person, a callous youth called Frankie, who makes his life a misery. Patrick's lucidity is of very little help: "Half of him saw and understood what Frankie was, so that he was twice the victim—of his own perceptiveness and of Frankie's capriciousness and greed" (228). His whole life is spent waiting for his capricious lover while constantly trying to find excuses for him. He rarely goes out for fear of missing Frankie: "But sometimes miracles happened, and for that reason he stayed in the flat, refused invitations, glanced at the clock, peeped through the curtains at the street beneath, and listened for footsteps" (106).

Neither Patrick nor Meg have the courage to break free from the hopeless situations in which they find themselves. Viewed as victims of a certain determinism, prisoners of their own fates, they simply endure their lives. The conviction of their helplessness, which Taylor conveys throughout her novel, contributes to the impression of gloom that emanates from the book. Taylor's touch is so light, however, that it never becomes oppressive.

The Soul of Kindness fully illustrates Taylor's central theme of isolation and loneliness. As their situation makes it impossible for the characters in the novel to relate to one another, they find themselves in complete isolation. In this novel, the inescapability of loneliness is made clearer than before. Patrick Barlow chooses to spend Christmas alone, rather than with Meg, in the hope that Frankie will come and see him. "Patrick was lonely. In the morning, he went to church and, after that, tried to forget the nature of the day. It should be possible, he decided, to ignore the dismal Christmas scene outside, groups of people homing fast, back to mother and father, until they were all cooped up in their families, leaving the streets deserted" (103). In the drab little house in Towersey, which she bought following Patrick's advice, Meg spends much time alone, too, having no friend apart from Flora, and finding it difficult to relate to her younger brother Kit.

The most striking illustration of loneliness in the novel may well be Elinor Pringle, the neglected wife of a M.P., who tries to fill her solitude with a variety of hobbies. She attempts to strike a friendship with her neighbor, Richard, whose company she enjoys. Richard is not very responsive and their casual relationship is therefore full of constraints. Richard wonders aloud: " 'It must be lonely for you.' She faced this warily. She wanted his sympathy; she wanted to indulge herself, angle for it, luxuriate in it; but she guessed that it might be a mistake, and perhaps a deadly one. Cautiously she said, 'I am rather used to it, you know' " (175). Elinor seems to have been created for the sole purpose of illustrating Taylor's concern with failed relationships and the ensuing loneliness. "He's really my only friend, she thought. How dreadful if I did something to lose him. It was all she wanted, and had happened with miraculous luck—to talk, to sit and have a drink with him, for him to be at ease with her, to take her for granted. She had not fallen in love with him and desired nothing that belonged to Flora; but he must have something left over from that, which he could spare to her; everybody has *something* left over" (173).

The answer to that last plea is negative; people have very little to offer each other. Isolated by their misery, or by their egotism, they are incapable of true relationships. *The Soul of Kindness* is indeed a pessimistic novel which allows itself little hope for human beings to help and solace each other. Brigid Brophy writes: "I value very highly indeed the considered and considerable despair at its heart."[6] Taylor, nevertheless, shows a commendable restraint and never lets her pessimistic views become unbearably oppressive.

The Wedding Group

In *The Wedding Group*, Taylor deals once again with the havoc that well-meaning people bring to the lives of others. She centers her story on a young girl, Cressida McPhail, who escapes from a stifling little community ruled by her grandfather, the despotic Harry Bretton, to find a place for herself in what she sees as the real world. Cressy then marries David Little, a confirmed bachelor, and falls under the influence of his possessive mother, Midge. The novel, following the development of the young couple's marital difficulties, focuses on Midge's constant interference which becomes increasingly nefarious.

Elizabeth Taylor contrasts two very different family groups. Harry Bretton and his family live an austere, frugal life, while Midge Little and her son David share a comfortable cottage and enjoy gourmet food, drinks, and evenings out. Both families share a common trait, nevertheless: they are ruled by two egotistical, manipulative characters. Harry Bretton imposes a certain way of life on his family, while Midge Little keeps her only remaining son under tight—if subtle—control. The irony of Cressy's situation is acute: she rebels against her grandfather's authority and finds her freedom, only to fall under the influence of cunning Midge who is shown as more harmful to her than Harry Bretton could ever be. If Cressy appears strong in her rebellion at Quayne, she is seen as weak and defenseless in the real world for she does not suspect its snares: "Cressy fought that battle with her grandfather, but this one she'll never fight. She doesn't even know there's a war."[7]

The novel is divided into two parts. The first part relates Cressy's escape from Quayne, her first steps in the outside world, and her getting acquainted with the Littles. The second part describes the consequences of her choice: her marriage to David Little and the subsequent difficulties developing under Midge's vigilant eye. The conclusion, with its customary ambiguous note, sees the young couple escaping to London and struggling to save their shaky marriage.

Taylor's short novel presents two distinct worlds. Harry Bretton's is an arts-and-crafts Catholic community based on a family unit which he keeps under tight control, allowing very little freedom to its members who, out of either apathy or indifference, do not dispute his authority. The tribe, as it is referred to, consists mostly of women. The men in the community, husbands chosen by Harry for his three daughters, are of no account: "As they had been acquired after the conversion, they were of the proper faith" (6).

The small community is somewhat medieval in style. Although it is ruled by Harry Bretton, it is, in fact, run by the women alone. When Cressy leaves school, her mother imparts her new goal to her: "To be a part of a busy, useful, self-sufficing community, her mother had said. This meant helping to bake bread, hoeing the kitchen garden, weaving dress lengths. The good life" (5). Paradoxically, in important matters, the women are allowed very little say. Their lives have been predetermined by their father. Cressy's mother finds her daughter's rebellion incomprehensible since her own father has always dictated her very thoughts: "Because her life at Quayne had been so right for her, she blamed herself, and not Quayne, that her daughter was at variance with it. She herself had been so contented. Her father had found for her, and kept for her, a beloved husband. She had never been parted from those she loved" (45). The condescension with which Harry Bretton treats women irks Cressy most of all and causes her to defy her irate grandfather.

Harry Bretton, the patriarch, is described with a great deal of irony. He is presented as a complacent man who feigns humility but reveres his own person and loves the sound of his own voice. Insisting on being called "the Master," he has his own biographer and deplores the fact that he has never been awarded a peerage. He has created Quayne partly in the hope of being thought of as controversial. His inordinate vanity makes him regard all painters as potential rivals. Turner is "safely dead," but Picasso is still alive at the time: "Over the years, he had come to hate Picasso, with a deep, uneasy hatred. He had always detested his work, but now he also detested the creator of it. He was envious of him for remaining, as he himself had not, a controversial figure. To have once been a controversial figure was something to look back on, and to know that he no longer was—or only to the elderly—humiliated him" (170). His controversial paintings consist of religious characters in modern dress and contemporary settings, and he usually uses his family as models. His work also betrays his disproportionate self-love. Cressy, who is examining a painting of the marriage at Cana, slyly notices that "Christ had a distinct look of Harry about Him" (52).

The Master is described as always knowing what is best for his family. By cutting them off from the outside world, he protects them against its artificiality and ugliness. "Here, there was nothing he thought of as spurious, nothing meretricious, nothing counterfeit. All was wholesome, necessary, simple; therefore good and beautiful, too" (7).

This chosen way of life, which he finds beneficial to himself, is imposed upon others who do not have the energy to fight. The Master's dogmatism tramples them into submission. "He harangued us all endlessly, about humility in art, humility in life. It's what he's got, he implied. No one else spoke, all the way down the table. Too humble, I suppose. They just went on eating beans; heard it all a thousand times before. Only the tame priest tried to put in a word or two, and then the Master took the chance to down some food, chewed and swallowed like mad, and then was at the ready again" (13).

Quayne is presented as a romantic notion, a utopia fantasized by its founder, a little world with no bearing on reality. Harry Bretton keeps it cut off from the outside world to avoid its corruption. Quayne stands on a hill, a signpost "Quayne Only" outlining its total isolation. Sheltered from the outside world, its members allow themselves to behave in a righteous manner. David Little is not received kindly as a prospective husband for Cressy. He shocks her mother deeply by his admission that his parents are separated: "He might as well have thrown in bankruptcy, syphilis, congenital madness, haemophilia, indecent exposure, treason, and fraud. From the expression on her face, it seemed no more could make a difference to Rose" (95). Yet the little community fails in its aspiration to holiness simply because the corruption comes from within, from Harry himself. Despite the fact that Harry presents himself as a strict theologian who enjoys reading—and commenting on—Aquinas, he superbly dismisses the fact that his best friend—and biographer— has made his granddaughter pregnant, finding it useful to have a young mother-to-be as a model for his painting. The pregnancy of Cressy's cousin, despite Harry's imperviousness to it, is seen as the beginning of the crumbling of the well-guarded facade: "Perhaps the rot of all time was setting in" (114). Cressy's rebellion is viewed as another flaw. She is aware that, by rejecting her religion, she is rejecting Quayne itself: "She knew that she was about to become—if it had not happened already— the one flaw in the Way of Life, the first blemish upon Quayne. Something which did not hold good, which ruined the argument" (7). Cressy's rebellious attitude is shown as destroying the perfect harmony that characterizes Quayne: "Poor little Cressy! She can't sing in tune with us any longer" (43). Cressy is consequently seen "in a harsh and ugly light—her distorted face, her clumsy rage, and, now, her discordant voice" (43). Yet there is little doubt in the reader's mind that Cressy's rebellion is a healthy positive reaction against her grandfather's stifling autocracy. Her one goal is to free herself from his tyranny and find a place for herself in the outside world.

Ironically, the outside, or "real," world, is represented by the village down the hill where Midge Little and her son, David, live. Cressy has always dreamed of "Wimpy Bars and a young man with a sports car, of cheap and fashionable clothes that would fall apart before she tired of them" (7). What paradoxically attracts the rebel from Quayne may not be the best features of our civilization. Discarding hand-woven fabrics, hand-made leather shoes, and wholesome food, Cressy longs for cheap clothing, plastic sandals, "synthetic custard and tinned spaghetti."

Cressy's naiveté, her curiosity and wonder in her discovery of this new world delight her new friends Midge and David Little. They introduce her to drinks, television—to which she soon becomes addicted—dancing, gourmet food, and pastry. Taylor describes the slow downfall of her young heroine who is not ready to fight the lure of the world. Her sheltered life has not prepared her for the pitfalls she is now encountering. She slowly becomes lazy, slovenly, negligent, and irresponsible. Whereas she was strong in her rebellion at Quayne, she is shown as weak as soon as she steps out of her sheltered world.

The world to which Cressy instinctively turns is not a sophisticated world. For the first time, Taylor does not resist the urge of being "contemporary": She paints an astonishing picture of lower-middle-class life in contemporary England, offering, for example, surprising descriptions of Wimpy Bars: "All those youths with studded leather jackets; ghastly smell of fried onions" (75). And as she describes her young heroine's enthusiasm for the prefabricated aspects of contemporary culture, Taylor continues her dispirited comments. She seems to share David's concealed disgust:

He looked with horror at a caseful of curled up fish in batter, at bright yellow cakes covered with shaggy coconut.
In front of them were black-coated, very much studded, motor-

bike boys, all wet, but docile. Cressy seemed to go mad in her enthusiasm, helping herself to a pork pie, a cheese roll, little packets of
Ry-vita and butter, a jelly with a very white whirl of cream on top,
and a cardboard beaker of coffee. David marvelled at her appetite.
He took a sausage-roll and coffee, and they found a table which had
just been wiped down, its sauce bottles regrouped, and its ash-tray
emptied.
The noise was deafening. (185)

Like Cressy, Midge Little belongs perfectly in Taylor's contemporary world. A woman in perfect accordance with her time,
an indefatigable dancer, she drinks gin, wears pink velvet trou-
sers, and goes to pubs by herself.

Taylor's characters drink a fair amount. The importance of
drinks in contemporary fiction is worth noting for it has become
a leitmotiv. On the one hand, it betrays a certaine "malaise":
Midge drinks to escape loneliness and fear, David to fill the
vacuum of his life. "Drink isn't really all I think about. It just
makes a sort of pattern in one's life, as other things don't seem
to" (92). On the other hand, it is used as a means of social
identification. One may remember Jim Dixon's famous outburst:
"Do I look as if I can afford spirits?"[8] Taylor's characters drink
spirits or wine, which betrays their social status and income
bracket. Within the spirit-drinking class, however, there are categories. Midge's gin-drinking seems a significant fact on which
Taylor slyly comments: "I never thought gin was quite the
thing—common sort of drink, like most of those who take it"
(28).

As part of her description of the contemporary world, Taylor
paints a depressing picture of married life. To please Midge,
Cressy and David move to a nearby cottage in the depths of
the country. The isolated cottage is a constant source of trouble.
In the winter, pipes freeze, telephone wire comes down, water
leaks through the roof. Cressy is quite incapable of coping with
her new responsibilities. She can neither cook nor clean and
David mourns his lost comfort. Taylor's descriptions are sharply
evocative of their struggles and extremely realistic, in her best
vein: "Cressy's room was like a stage-set for some depressing
play about young-married strife, the very background for bicker-
ing and disillusion. Diapers steamed round the fire; the ironing-

board was piled high with unironed clothes, and the table with unwashed crockery" (160). Taylor's intimations of the pitfalls of married life ring true; the reader witnesses the rapid disintegration of David's marriage, who had married somewhat in haste.

The Wedding Group illustrates Taylor's ability to describe scenes from the lives of the English middle class. It may be the most English of her novels. Taylor has earned a reputation for her keen social awareness as well as her acute psychological perception. One reviewer notes: "It is part of her considerable insight into the English middle-class that she recognizes and accepts the way violent emotions and vicious antagonisms almost never surface, but fester beneath a compromise of insincerity and good manners."9

The Wedding Group shows a perfectly smooth surface. Its tone is quiet, even, tasteful. Crises are never loud, nor scenes vociferous. When Rose is told that her only daughter is going to be married at a registry office, the shock and sorrow that she feels are noticeably toned down: "And then Rose moved to a chair and sat down, thinking her legs would support her no longer" (95). The underlying drama of David's announcement to his mother Midge is barely apparent. The smooth surface of their relationship is hardly rippled, even though wild emotions rage inside: "She, like Rose, turned aside for a moment, and she put her glass down before she took a sip" (96).

Taylor also allows her characters some very restrained, understated, "English" reactions. To David's proposal of marriage, Cressy immediately replies: "But are you sure I shan't be an inconvenience to you?" (92). When he decides to tell his former girl friend Nell, her reaction is also exceptionally quiet: "Well, I'm looking forward to my tea" (94). There are no great scenes in *The Wedding Group*. Cressy's tears, of which she is prodigal, are the only outward signs of emotion.

There are, however, violent emotions brewing under the civilized, constrained surface. Midge, who lives alone, having been deserted by her husband and ignored by her two other sons, has concentrated all her love and hopes on her youngest son David. She now strives to be what she never was in the past: a perfect wife, mother, hostess, and companion. Fearful of solitude and of losing her only son, she tries to make his home

life as pleasant as she can: "He thought of his home as one
that had always run smoothly, revolving about him, where his
friends came often, and liked to come, for Midge was a perfect
hostess-mother, easy, undemanding, kept young by her enthusi-
asms, ready to try everything, learn everything" (15).

Midge's fear of being once again abandoned is so strong that
she is shown as constantly on her guard, always under tight
control. She makes a point of never asking too many questions,
of never irking her son in any way. She is consequently presented
as sly, scheming, and calculating. Yet Taylor passes no judgment
on her character. She describes Midge with mild sympathy, fair-
ness, objectivity, merely relating her ambiguous actions. A critic
wrote: "But it is perhaps Mrs. Taylor's greatest talent as a novelist that combined with an often withering disgust for hypocrisy
and self-delusion (that peculiarly English characteristic) she
shows enormous sympathy and generosity towards it."[10]

Taylor's treatment of her character is so subtle and discreet
that readers may have difficulty assessing Midge's part in controlling the events which occur in the novel. Yet it seems that
Midge plays a very discreet deus-ex-machina. In order to keep
David and Cressy under her control, Midge finds them a little
cottage close to her house. She also senses that, by encouraging
marital strife, she stands a better chance of getting her own
way. As she knows all of Cressy's present and future weaknesses,
she subtly encourages her laziness, gluttony, and negligence.
Paradoxically, she also tries to make life pleasant for them, in-
vites them to dinner, brings gifts whenever she comes to see
them. As winter gets more severe and the young couple's discomfort increases, Midge's fears grow. She soon feels compelled
to stage a burglary in her own home to make her son feel the
weight of his responsibilities toward his mother. Diamond ear-
rings allegedly disappear; yet their later reappearance in a jar
of rice provides the turning point of the story by finally freeing
David from his mother's clutches.

It is hard, nevertheless, to dislike Midge, for Taylor paints
a rather endearing picture of the sly, gin-drinking grandmother.
It remains true that, behind the kindness, the generosity, there
lies self-protectiveness and self-interest. Midge's deviousness,
however, is made to appear much more attractive than the cold
virtuousness of Cressy's mother. Even Midge's possessiveness

is presented as a forgivable trait rather than the destructive trend it actually is.

Taylor does not treat David so kindly. He impersonates the conflict of loyalties which is at the core of the novel. David deceives himself about his mother, refusing to acknowledge her possessiveness and deviousness. Yet even though he dismisses his friends' remarks about umbilical cords and apron strings, he feels a certain amount of uneasiness which becomes perceptible when he broaches the subject of his marrying Cressy. David resents the burden of responsibilities which has weighed on him all his life. Since his marriage to Cressy, he is torn between the dual responsibilities of his mother and new family. David's dream of living in London, close to his work and friends, springs largely from his hope of then being able to shake off his moral duties toward both Cressy and his mother. The sudden realization of his mother's deviousness sets him free and gives a chance to his faltering marriage.

The novel deals largely with self-delusion. Very little ever comes to the surface. Pretenses are kept, good manners prevail. Taylor remains self-effacing, detached, and discreet. Her characters show little self-awareness or lucidity; nor are they given to denunciations or self-reproach. Each crisis which arises solves itself smoothly.

Giving the novel its title, the "wedding group" is the brief union of the two families, of two irreconcilable worlds, with Harry Bretton, for once, not in the middle but on the side. Reminding the reader of Ivy Compton Burnett's family groups, Taylor's group is also dominated by tensions, behind civilized, polite appearances. The novel's title also refers to a Wedgwood bridal group which Cressy painstakingly buys for Midge who had admired it. It later gets broken heedlessly, a symbol of David and Cressy's shaky marriage.

Once again, Taylor is perhaps a little too succinct in her novel writing. She hints at side issues yet does not develop them. Too much is left unsaid. A reviewer writes: "She procrastinates on plot, and her characters seem to have few resources beyond gardening."[11] Taylor hastily sketches a few secondary characters. For example, the reader is briefly introduced to the charwoman, the picturesque Mrs. Brindle, who works at Quayne and at Midge's and acts as a go-between: "Mrs. Brindle was well-known as a tower of strength. She knew it, and the knowledge spurred her on to greater efforts" (47). David's father also appears briefly now and then, but his solitariness is not dwelt upon. Little is known of David's life outside his home. An intriguing pair, Toby and his sister Alexia, friends of David's, share a few moments with him. Taylor hints at David's attraction for the beautiful Alexia yet does not pursue what could have been a fascinating topic: "It would be more wicked, David thought, still watching Alexia's intent face, really much more wicked, than stealing another man's wife" (36). One reviewer epitomizes the problem that the reader encounters in several of Taylor's novels: "Perhaps this is an inevitable criticism of any writer who excels at short stories; Mrs. Taylor economizes and sketches where she might have squandered some loaded paint-brushes."[12]

Both *The Soul of Kindness* and *The Wedding Group* center on a well-meaning character who, consciously or not, manipulates others. Midge Little has been called "Flora grown older and more mischievous."[13] The connection, however, does not do justice to Midge who has, at least, a certain amount of self-awareness. Despite her weaknesses, Midge appears as a credible character and contrasts with bland, flawless Flora; nor does Midge arouse the same uneasiness as Flora does. The connection lies in the egotism of the two characters who do good for their own gratification.

Both novels could be seen as "novels of exposure" as they satirize a certain category of people. Taylor, however, makes it clear that she is not attacking the general but the individual. Her mild satire has no reformative purpose. It is human nature, in all its facets, which interests her. Taylor's skill lies in dramatizing—not exposing—the idiosyncrasies of her characters.

Chapter Seven

The Melodramatic Mood
of the Seventies

With her last two novels, *Mrs Palfrey at the Claremont* (1972) and *Blaming* (1976), Taylor comes as close to being "contemporary" as she could ever be. Both novels show a relentless concern with death and also reveal a form of subdued anger that had not been apparent in Taylor's earlier fiction. The novels' melodramatic content, reflective of the current trend of the English novel, is also more perceptible than before, in spite of Taylor's long-established restraint and sobriety. The quiet pathos that characterizes *Mrs Palfrey at the Claremont* may make it Taylor's best novel. *Blaming,* on the other hand, is a more confused novel that reflects a conflict of loyalties and a consequent shifting in Taylor's clearly expressed moral sense.

Mrs Palfrey at the Claremont

Mrs Palfrey at the Claremont is a fascinating novel about old age, its loneliness and its indignities. It could have been called "They Aren't Allowed to Die There," the title which young Ludovic Mayers chooses for his own novel, running parallel to Taylor's story. The matter-of-fact title selected by Taylor emphasizes her desire not to indulge in easy sentimentality. Her description of old age remains brisk, objective, extremely amusing at times, but also pessimistic in a subtle, less clearly defined way. The symbolic setting—a hotel in London—the handful of lonely and neglected elderly people, all conspire to create an atmosphere of resigned doom. Taylor's objectivity and detachment do not prevent her from conveying discreet pathos throughout the novel. *Mrs Palfrey at the Claremont* epitomizes her talent as a novelist: it displays a mixture of sensitive observation, detached pathos, and subtle wit.

Taylor has chosen a particularly interesting setting for her eleventh novel. She sets her story at the Claremont, a second-rate hotel that advertises "Reduced winter rates. Excellent cuisine," thus attracting lonely and slightly impoverished genteel old people. Its location on the Cromwell Road, South Kensington, a district well known for its transient aspect, adds an ephemeral quality to its grim circumstances. The Claremont is also situated in a part of London that abounds in such establishments. Taylor's hotel is given a symbolical significance for it is a place of transit between life and death. Residents arrive, promising themselves that they need not stay for long. The irony of their situation is obvious: as they have nowhere else to go, their only option is to move to another, perhaps slightly worse, hotel until the time comes for the nursing home where they are allowed to die.

Taylor chooses circumstances as dreary as she can to describe her protagonist's arrival: "Mrs Palfrey first came to the Claremont Hotel on a Sunday afternoon in January. Rain had closed in over London, and her taxi sloshed along the almost deserted Cromwell Road, past one cavernous porch after another, the driver going slowly and poking his head into the wet, for the hotel was not known to him."[1] A feeling of imprisonment begins to dominate Mrs. Palfrey's mood when she steps into her room: "When the porter had put down her suitcases and gone, she thought that prisoners must feel as she did now the first time they are left in their cell, first turning to the window, then facing about to stare at the closed door: after that, counting paces from wall to wall" (5).

As old age resembles childhood in its dependence upon others, Taylor establishes a revealing parallel between hotel life and school life. A handful of residents has established its own little rules to which the newcomer must abide. When one of the long-term residents speaks to her for the first time, Mrs. Palfrey feels like "a new girl at school addressed for the first time by a prefect" (7). The fact that someone has spoken to her, thus breaking the isolation in which she stands, childishly touches Mrs. Palfrey: "Someone had spoken to her: she had a name to remember" (8). Later, she feels proud to be asked to run errands for crippled Mrs. Arbuthnot and fervently hopes to become part of the little group.

The Claremont group is mainly identified by its little rituals practiced daily in the dining room. The reading of the menu, an hour or so before lunch and dinner, constitutes the highlight of the day and offers them a little choosing and a mild sense of adventure as their life once had.

It is in these rituals that Mrs. Palfrey soon finds herself trapped. As life is dull at the Claremont, the residents feel a great deal of curiosity for each other's outside lives, personified by visitors. Having thoughtlessly mentioned the presence in London of her grandson, Desmond, Mrs. Palfrey soon becomes an object of pity when Desmond does not appear, in spite of her renewed invitations. As a result, she finds herself embroiled in many face-saving deceptions. Her accidental meeting with a poor would-be writer, Ludovic Mayers, results in a misunderstanding—Ludo being mistaken for her grandson and she shamefacedly failing to correct her entourage. The deception is carried a step further when she starts regarding—and treating—Ludo as her grandson. The late appearance of her real grandson, a callous youth, does little to deter her, and she quickly gets him out of the way, partly to protect her little subterfuge, and partly because she now sees Desmond for what he is: "She could find no patience for this pompous grandson; her love lay elsewhere" (105).

In *Mrs Palfrey at the Claremont,* Taylor achieves remarkable success with the characterization of her dignified protagonist. Mrs. Palfrey's name is a clear indication of the way Taylor sees her aging heroine—proud, dignified and reliable like a parade horse. She even allows one of her characters to make an appropriate joke: "Mrs Palfrey is a dark horse" (41). Mrs. Palfrey is the incarnation of "the spirit of the Empire builders." A bastion of the British Empire, she is seen as representing a class—and a world—in the process of disappearing. Taylor describes her with considerable sympathy, not always precluding amusement, however. A distinguished, imposing woman, she is portrayed as not particularly feminine either in looks or outlook: "She was a tall woman with big bones and a noble face, dark eyebrows and a neatly folded jowl. She would have made a distinguished-looking man and, sometimes, wearing evening-dress, looked as Lord Louis Mountbatten might in drag" (4). Mrs. Palfrey's strict upbringing has taught her the value of sto-

icism and dignity, and the importance of never giving up. When
she feels depression closing in, she exhorts herself to courage:
"I shall be able to watch the lilacs coming out, she thought.
It will be just like the garden at Rottingdean. The setting could
scarcely have been more different; but she felt a determination
about the lilac trees. They were to be a part of her rules, her
code of behaviour. Be independent; never give way to melancholy; never touch capital. And she had abided by the rules"
(10).

Mrs. Palfrey represents the old world's dignity; she has
staunch principles and a mind of her own: " 'I speak as I find'
might have been her motto, if she had not thought it servants'
parlance" (13). Accustomed to facing up to any situation, however embarrassing, Mrs. Palfrey nevertheless finds it a great
strain to cover up for her grandson's rudeness. She feels forced
to lie, then to remember her lies. She also has to go against
her principles when she agrees to loan Ludo money out of capital. Then, an accident obliges her to touch capital again, much
to her chagrin, in order to be moved out of the geriatric ward
into a private room.

Taylor describes Mrs. Palfrey as a typical illustration of England's older conservative generation who, having barely sur-
vived the war, struggle to settle down in the dire conditions
of postwar Britain. Like most of Taylor's protagonists, Mrs. Palfrey feels great melancholy about the past. Taylor hints, once
more, at the solidity and certainty found in the past, whereas
the shifting present has nothing comparable to offer. Because of
her age, Mrs. Palfrey has a special place in Taylor's fictional
world. She is the only character who, looking back, remembers:
"When she was young, it had seemed that nearly all the world
was pink in her school atlas—'ours,' in fact. Nearly all ours!
she had thought. Pink was the colour, and the word, of well-
being, and of optimism. To be born into it was the greatest
luck" (91).

In spite of her pioneer spirit, Mrs. Palfrey knows that she
must be flexible. She is also aware that "life was changed, and
to save her sanity she must change with it" (15). Her accidental
meeting with Ludo opens new vistas for her. She discovers that
some know penury and receive no help from the "old boys'
network." She becomes aware that people actually live in base-

ment flats: "She could glimpse bed-sitting rooms—like Ludo's, some of them—where once cooks had attended ranges, rattling dampers, cooking off hot-plates, skimming stock-pots, while listening to house-maid's gossip brought from above stairs" (56). It is not an easy task for someone of Mrs. Palfrey's background to imagine life below stairs. She experiences a feeling of bewilderment, a loss of sense of direction: "Some of the basement windows were covered by vertical iron bars, so that it must be like being in prison to live behind them, she thought. One could peer up at feet going by, and the wheels of cars; but no sky, only the stuccoed wall of the area, the dead leaves blown there, a fern growing out of a crack in the plaster, or moss covering bricks; dustbins; or a row of flower-pots containing old earth, but no longer anything growing" (56).

Mrs. Palfrey's feelings of affection for Ludo do not stop her from viewing the younger generation with much distrust. She is relieved to feel that Ludo could never be seen carrying a banner or throwing a paving stone: "He seemed to believe in nothing, and she was glad of this" (46). Her preference, conveyed by Taylor, for an absence of belief is a sad indication of the general demoralization and helplessness that have undermined the old "Empire builders" spirit.

The friendship that develops between the purposeful old woman and the drifting young man is refreshing, even though they both, in a sense, make use of each other. Ludo uses Mrs. Palfrey as a source of material for a novel he is writing about old people; she uses Ludo to impersonate her grandson when he fails to come and see her. Soon, however, Mrs. Palfrey starts feeling like a young girl in love. When Ludo innocently tells her about his girl friend Rosy, Mrs. Palfrey feels sharp pangs of jealousy. Taylor even compares her to "a frantic, left wife." As for Ludo, who frequently feels like an orphan, meeting Mrs. Palfrey seems a stroke of luck.

In spite of their friendship, they are extreme opposites, however. Mrs. Palfrey, a symbol of old England, of traditions, has outlived a good marriage, has cared and looked after her only daughter. Ludo, the product of welfare state education and a broken home, is the son of a woman of "lose morals and, worse than that, untidy thinking." Paradoxically, Mrs. Palfrey is neglected by her daughter and ignored by her grandson whereas

Ludo behaves as a loving son to his helpless mother. Ludo has never known anyone like Mrs. Palfrey, "no spoiling aunt or comfortable Nannie, no doting elder sisters" (83). Their friendship suggests the fact that perhaps the two worlds are not quite irreconcilable.

Briefly, yet incisively, Taylor offers the reader a description of the little group of elderly people who are ending their lives at the Claremont. They serve mostly as character foils to Mrs. Palfrey. It soon becomes clear that Taylor's heroine has little in common with them. Mrs. Burton's lack of moderation and taste only underlines Mrs. Palfrey's poise and self-control. Mrs. Post's silliness and heedlessness stress Mrs. Palfrey's sense of responsibility and independence. Mr. Osmond's salacious mind contrasts unfavorably with Mrs. Palfrey's reserve and dignity. In fact, Ludo endears himself greatly to Mrs. Palfrey when he asks with genuine concern: "Are they all that nice? Are they nice enough for *you*, I mean?" (74). Mr. Osmond admires Mrs. Palfrey a great deal and, after inviting her to be his guest at a Masonic dinner, suddenly proposes to her, to her deep embarrassment. Later in the story, her desire to escape from his attentions causes her to rush off and fall down a flight of stairs, an accident that proves fatal to her.

Besides showing different facets of Mrs. Palfrey's character, the Claremont residents are also used by Taylor to offer a dispirited study of old age. Kingsley Amis writes: "The principal subject of the novel is loneliness, old age and approaching death, and I must warn those who dislike this triad of prospects that they will not like it any better on finishing [this novel]."[2] Taylor describes the desultory lonely lives of the Claremont residents who have chosen London over Brighton or Bournemouth to be close to relatives who, in effect, do not care for them. Aware that they are little more than burdens to the younger generations, the old people are nevertheless involved in constant self-deception: " 'Relations make all the difference,' Mrs Post said. 'Although one would never make a home with them' " (11). Mrs. Palfrey feels that the letters she exchanges with her daughter are a mere formality. She therefore finds herself in complete isolation; the burden of widowhood has to be borne alone: "Although she felt too old to do so, she knew that she must soldier on, as Arthur might have put it, with this new life of her own. She would never again have anyone to turn to for help, to take her arm crossing a road, to comfort her; to listen to any news of hers, good or bad" (163).

It is a grim study of old age which Taylor presents. Her characters know—even if they rarely admit it—that they have little to offer to a society that worships youth: "As one gets older life becomes all take and no give. One relies on other people for the treats and things. It's like being an infant again" (113). Taylor establishes a dispiriting parallel between old age and infancy, showing how life begins and ends in complete dependency upon others. The essential difference is bitter to face, too: infants are loved whereas old people are resented. "It was hard work being old. It was like being a baby, in reverse. Every day for an infant means some new little thing learned; every day for the old means some little thing lost" (159). Taylor's treatment of her elderly characters is sympathetic yet she remains detached and matter-of-fact, just as Ludo, who favors George Gissing, immediately jots down some notes after rescuing Mrs. Palfrey from a nasty fall: "fluffy grey knickers . . . elastic . . . veins on leg colour of grapes . . . smell of lavender water (ugh!) . . . big spots on back of shiny hands and more veins . . . horizontal wrinkles across hands" (28).

One of the most interesting aspects of Taylor's treatment of old age can perhaps be found in the way the notion of time affects her elderly characters who have little more to expect but death. Even though their present lives are lonely and dull, they cling to it with desperation: "It was another Sunday wrested from the geriatric ward, she told herself" (45). Time for the elderly goes slowly; it is always earlier than they had thought. Mrs. Palfrey attempts to do all her daily tasks slowly so that "later might seem sooner." The present moment means nothing to Taylor's characters. Strangely enough, they do not seem to live in the past either, but look forward to some brighter future, blinding themselves to the fact that it holds nothing for them but increasing deterioration of body and mind, and death. In the emptiness of their lives, the knowledge that time goes by sustains them. Taylor hints at a conflictual desire to escape from their dreary existence while wishing to retain it at all costs. It is, in fact, in an attempt to escape from the pressures of closed-in life at the Claremont that Mrs. Palfrey rushes out, stumbles, and falls, an accident that costs her her life.

Throughout the novel, Taylor conveys an impression of ap-

palled despair, comparable to Mrs. Palfrey's first impression on
setting foot inside the Claremont. Taylor's heroine, who fights
depression with all her inner strength, considers herself an optimist. She nevertheless admits—a feeling Taylor probably
shares—"how deeply pessimistic one must be in the first place,
to need the sort of optimism she now had at her command"
(85). It is the existentialist optimism of those who have nothing
to lose.

Mrs Palfrey at the Claremont is a fascinating example of Taylor's
perfected technique. In spite of her detachment and apparent
lack of involvement in her own story, Taylor manages to convey
the compassion she feels for the particular plight of the elderly.
The novel is witty and amusing at times, yet none of the characters are ever seen as grotesque or farcical. Taylor treats a delicate
topic with great sensitivity and dignity.

Blaming

Published posthumously by Taylor's husband, Blaming derives
a certain significance from being Taylor's last novel and from
being written so close to the end of her life. In spite of its
shortness, the novel appears complete and has polish. It is an
interesting piece of work, which seems to tie together all the
loose ends in Taylor's fiction and bring her career as a novelist
to a dignified ending. Like Mrs Palfrey at the Claremont, the
novel deals with death but it is more particularly concerned
with the burden of grief and remorse which those who die
leave upon the living, and with the cocoon of self-protection
with which the living attempt to surround themselves. Characterized by latent pessimism, Blaming reflects the author's dejected
mood, yet Taylor's ever-present and largely compelling sense
of humor livens up what would otherwise be a somewhat depressing novel.

Once again, Taylor casts a painter and a novelist as her protagonists. Even though she kills Nick Henderson off in the first
chapter, Taylor attaches some importance to his talent as a
painter for it allows some useful insight into the personality
of his wife Amy, her main protagonist. Taylor also draws an
interesting parallel between Nick and Frances, the artist in A
Wreath of Roses. Both share the same dedication to details and

the desire to paint people in their true settings. Nick's portrait of Amy is revealing of the way she is to be seen: "A very young Amy had been painted sitting on a bare staircase of knotted wood with rows of nails; dusty sunshine fell over her from an uncurtained window on a landing. There was nothing but stairs, banister, window and walls, and Amy very small, like a child, sitting hunched-up, her arms round her knees, her face pale and anxious-looking below a fringe of dark hair."[3] The choice of a staircase as Amy's true setting is indicative of her childlike personality, for staircases are traditionally associated with children. Amy has the self-absorption of a child and the same reliance upon others.

Nick's creativity is also used by Taylor to give unity to her fictional world. Like Frances in *A Wreath of Roses,* Nick decides to stop painting when, after a long illness, he loses his grip on life. His last unfinished painting on the easel is strangely reminiscent of Frances's last one: "It was of some old-fashioned creamy roses against a dark background" (160). The symbol of roses is a passing reference to Ophelia's last gesture before her death—namely, the relishing of her wreath of roses. As in the earlier novel, this chosen symbol unifies the narrative.

Taylor's amusing insight into the novelist's plight carries sly allusions to her own predicament. The characterization of Martha is only slightly veiled in this particular matter: "She was a novelist, an expatriate one at that, a writer of sad *contes* about broken love affairs, of depressed and depressing women. Her few books were handsomely printed, widely spaced on good paper, well-reviewed, and more or less unknown. Without fretting, she waited to be discovered" (14). Yet, in Martha, Taylor presents a novelist of a different style from her own. Martha's obsession with details, at the expense of characterization and plot, contrasts with Taylor's more pictorial form of expression. "Objects took the place of characters—the cracked plate, a dripping tap, a bunch of water-sprinkled violets minutely described, a tin of sardines, a broken comb; and the lone woman moved among them as if in a dream" (47). Even if the attention to carefully selected details is a trademark of Taylor's talent, she remains an impressionistic writer. Unlike George Gissing, to whom she implicitly compares herself at times, Taylor has no wish to describe the seediest aspects of life, but to present its most charming, picturesque facets. Martha's style, however, is viewed as indicative of her inquisitive, fastidious personality. After reading one of her novels, Amy admits to herself that she does not understand Martha's outlook. It is implied that Amy's lack of understanding stems from her lack of a grip on reality: "She had not known what to make of that book, the humourless study of sexuality, the desperate foray into a man's— a married man's—world, or, rather, a narrow aspect of it. The stresses and despair, and bloody-mindedness. No one had any money, but they managed to drink bourbon, wore racoon coats, travelled, or had travelled" (64–65). In fact, the ambiance of the novel—reminiscent of Sagan—is totally foreign to Amy, who has never experienced any such emotions or found herself in such an unfamiliar milieu.

Not unlike Martha's novel, *Blaming* is "a sad little story" about the various responsibilities which burden human beings. In her fictional world as a whole, Taylor, who does not believe in God, lays much stress upon solidarity between human beings as the upholding force in an otherwise meaningless world. Even though Taylor does not intrude in her narrative, she infuses *Blaming* with a strong moral sense reminiscent of Austen's. It is clear that, in her opinion, individuals have a moral duty to help each other. When they shirk their responsibilities, as Amy does, the weight of authorial disapproval is subtly but unequivocally felt. Constantly presented on a background of muddy waters—an appropriate setting—Amy is one of the most controversial of Taylor's heroines. A reviewer writes: "Taylor holds Amy's character against the light of a highly developed moral sense and finds her wanting."[4] Taylor sets out to prove how an apparently harmless woman can turn into a destructive creature when misfortunes strike her. Interestingly, Amy's destructiveness comes from her nonactions, her refusal to be drawn into others' lives. The brief acquaintance between Amy and Martha, struck during a Mediterranean cruise, develops when Nick suddenly dies of a heart attack. Martha selflessly gives up the rest of the cruise to rescue helpless Amy, yet her kindness meets little more than mild antagonism on Amy's part. Back in England, Amy is quick to banish the American girl from her mind as part of the nightmare through which she has just lived. Now that she is alone, Amy expects everyone to look after her—her son James, her housekeeper Ernie Pounce, her doctor and friend Gareth Lloyd. As a result, she resents any demand made upon either her time or sympathy. Taylor draws a parallel between grown-up Amy and her tyrannical four-year-old granddaughter Isobel. After describing Isobel as a despotic little monster, Taylor hints that Amy and she share the same compulsive egotism and self-absorption. Ironically, Amy does not care much for Isobel and prefers to spend time with docile, well-behaved seven-year-old Dora.

Amy's indifference to anyone's problems makes her one of the most selfish characters in Taylor's fiction. Martha is shocked by Amy's constant wish to protect her privacy and her lack of curiosity toward those around her: "You ask no questions. For instance, Ernie. You really know nothing about him, where he goes on his day off. I don't suppose you know that. Whereas I do, and a lot more besides. And also *me*. You know nothing about me, either—the sort of place where I live, the way I earn my living" (76). Amy is all too quick to dismiss Martha's increasing difficulties in dealing with her life. After an unsuccessful attempt at marriage, back in the States, Martha finally finds the courage to return to London, yet Amy heartlessly fails to meet her at the airport, arguing to herself that the taxi ride would be costly and, untruthfully, that Martha would prefer to settle in somewhere first. Martha's suicide, a few days later, shakes Amy up. Like Flora, in *The Soul of Kindness,* Amy faces up to her selfishness, wonders if she is to blame, and only revives when her friends assure her that she is in no way responsible for the tragedy:

"I did try," Amy said, running the tip of a finger under her eyes. "No one can say I didn't." But she knew that there were those who would.

"I'll say you tried."

"But I didn't do my best," she said bravely; trying out this statement, too.

"It was others that didn't do their best. That's as clear as a nutshell." (176).

Taylor focuses her last novel on the concept of "last gesture": death, its finality, and the consequences upon others. Two deaths occur in the novel: Nick's, in Istambul, early in the story; and Martha's, in London, at the end of the novel. Nick's death engineers the drama which is enacted in the novel by involving Amy, much against her will, in Martha's existence. Martha's suicide provides the climax of the novel by heaping a burden of responsibility on Amy and her husband Simon. Martha has married Simon and gone back to live in the States with him. Physically unwell and depressed by the intellectual and emotional vacuum in which she has had to live, Martha has longed for her old life in London and has dreamed of escaping. Amy plays a part in making it possible for Martha to fly back to London: she sends her a ticket bought with the money that Martha had thoughtfully left behind. Back in London with nowhere to go and no one to turn to, Martha succumbs to despair and kills herself in a squalid little hotel room near Paddington.

Taylor emphasizes the dramatically different reactions that reveal the personalities of her two protagonists. Amy, who has much to reproach herself with—having constantly let Martha down—feels brutally challenged in her sense of right and wrong, yet she immediately looks for someone to blame other than herself. She is careful to seek the support of those who are unlikely to blame her, such as her friend Gareth Lloyd: "And he would come and assure her that she was not to blame any more than anyone else; that there had been many assembling circumstances all contributing their share to the disaster" (177).

Opposite what she calls Amy's "ostrich" attitude, Taylor describes the remorse and guilt that righteous Simon displays to Amy's intense discomfort. Their confrontation, which cowardly Amy had tried to avoid, provides one of the dramatic highlights of the novel.

"I think she was a bit lonely at first. And wasn't awfully well, was she?"

Briefly, he brushed his forehead with his hand. "My fault again. I'm afraid I told her those headaches were just to punish me. Every time she did something wrong . . . I mean made a mistake, or acted in some way I could not understand or cope with, there were those headaches. I believed the doctor had talked her out of them."

He is a glutton for self-censure, Amy thought wearily. She said, "Dangerous, being talked out of illnesses. I blame your doctor for doing that." She was relieved—and Simon was relieved to hear it—to be able to say that there was blame lying elsewhere. (185–86)

Taylor betrays, in *Blaming,* a certain amount of subdued undi-
rected anger, perhaps at the way human beings keep failing
each other and avoiding their responsibilities toward each other.
Her anger becomes apparent in the ironic disparity between
Amy's peaceful words: "I think we'll just wait, and hope" (142)
and the grim outcome of the novel. Taylor allows self-deception
to prevail, yet Martha's last gesture appears as an unequivocal
condemnation of those who failed her.

If, in spite of its latent pessimism, *Blaming* remains easy to
read, it is largely due to Taylor's wit in describing the various
idiosyncrasies of her characters. Taylor draws a revealing parallel
between her two protagonists, Amy and Martha, contrasting
the foibles of an English woman with those of an American.
Amy's "Englishness" is much emphasized. "In spite of her assurance about clothes—that orange caftan, for instance—there was
something girlish about her, and Martha, openly staring at her
pale face (pale, for she never tanned, got only a scattering of
tiny freckles, like grated nutmeg), and at her dark fringed hair,
was trying to analyse this. Whatever was the cause, Amy seemed
to have remained at the age of seventeen, or thereabouts; but
it was the English girlhood of her own class and time. The
like never to come again, Martha, much younger and American,
decided. She loved Englishness" (16). Taylor presents Amy
as a typical product of English breeding. She remains cold and
reserved at all times. After Nick's death, Martha watches her
sitting alone, still and rigid, wearing a shady hat, sun-glasses,
and a pair of white cotton gloves: "It was as if she were trying
to cover as much of herself as possible" (30). The white cotton
gloves are the outward sign of Amy's forbidding attitude toward
others. Martha mistakes Amy's reserve and reticence for a na-
tional trait: "Another thing about the English, Martha noted;
they close up; they suddenly want to go home, or for you to.
She thought they must be the fastest givers-up in the world,
remembered wars, but dismissed that sort of tenacity as coming
from having had no choice" (68). Amy's apparently stoical attitude is not one of courage, however. She behaves with dignity
because she has been taught not to display emotions in public.
Inwardly, she is as panic stricken as a lost child. Like Mrs. Palfrey,
Amy represents a class—she is even referred to as "Memsahib."
Yet, unlike Mrs. Palfrey, she does not belong to the Empire
builders class. Accustomed to living in the shadow of a man,

pretending to herself that she is looking after him whereas he is, in fact, protecting her, Amy is incapable of fending for herself. Martha dimly senses that her friend belongs to a "dead race." When Amy later meets involved young couples who combine work with taking care of their family and busying themselves with social work, she feels stirrings of inadequacy. Taylor hints that Amy does not have much to show for her life, thus discreetly mocking Martha's serious assumption that Amy is "the English woman complete."

Taylor emphasizes the contrast between Amy's self-absorbed personality and Martha's generous nature. Martha represents impulsive and generous kindness—a trait that Taylor always describes as rare and valuable. In Istambul, Martha's company saved Amy from complete despair. "There had only been Martha, going on in her unexpected, unco-ordinated manner, pressing those figs on her when she could scarcely swallow her tears, making strange conversations on the plane, running round Istambul on errands, getting in touch with undertakers" (39). Her many kindnesses to Amy—in particular, her effort to track down one of Nick's early paintings—reveal a selfless generosity which embarrasses and shames Amy. Taylor constantly contrasts Martha's kindness toward Amy with Amy's pettiness toward her. Amy is blind to Martha's very real qualities because she can only see what meets the eye: that Martha is neither neat nor tidy; that she pays no heed to her appearances, wearing crumpled, torn blouses, shapeless sweaters, a dirty raincoat. Amy, who completely lacks curiosity about others' lives, also resents Martha's inquisitiveness. Martha's interest in other people makes her forget the social barriers that the English jealously guard. She shakes hands with Amy's housekeeper, Ernie, both to his delight and horror, then she goes to the kitchen to find out more about him, to Amy's extreme annoyance. Nevertheless, Amy notes that Martha shows little interest for houses or food or drink—matters of great importance to the English.

As a literary creation, Martha has been an object of controversy. According to a reviewer: "While Martha is around, *Blaming* is at its most brilliant."[5] Yet another notes: "The weak spot that blurs the book is Martha: although we learn of her tiresome, her generous and her ridiculous sides, these never quite fit together into one person."[6] Martha is always presented from Amy's point of view, and since Amy fails to "place" Martha, the impression conveyed is never quite clear. Moreover, Taylor's attitude toward both her protagonists is ambivalent too. She is pitiless toward Amy, mocking her good opinion of herself, deploring her lack of generosity and honesty. Yet even though she presents Martha as a better human being, it is somehow felt that she feels some deeply rooted sympathy for objectionable Amy. It may be Amy's Englishness that endears her to her creator while, with Martha, she may have created a character too outlandish for her own conservative tastes.

It may be Taylor's ambivalence toward her characters which makes *Blaming* a confusing novel. In spite of the assertion of a strong moral sense on the part of the author, there is, at times, a shifting in Taylor's loyalties which confuses the reader.

Blaming is also Taylor's "last gesture." It is a novel that remains eminently readable mostly through Taylor's skillful characterization. In spite of a superficial lightness of tone, its mood is pessimistic, however, and it provides a good but grim ending to Taylor's career as a novelist.

Chapter Eight
A Short-Story Writer

Elizabeth Taylor has earned, over the years, a solid reputation as a writer of short stories. Her stories which, for the most part, have been published in such magazines as the *New Yorker, Harper's Bazaar,* and *Harper's,* have also been collected into four volumes: *Hester Lilly, The Blush, A Dedicated Man,* and *The Devastating Boys.* This can be viewed as a homage to her talent, since collections of short stories are not reputed profitable business for publishers.

Taylor has commented at some length upon her technique as a short-story writer. Not unlike Virginia Woolf, Taylor lays much stress upon the idea of inspiration. Disregarding the notion of "the coming upon an idea," Taylor specifies: "Its coming upon the writer is how I think of it myself. It is completely different from the beginning of a novel, which is a conscious scheming. I believe that short stories are inspired—breathed in in a couple of breaths. For success there must be immediate impact, less going into anything, more suggestiveness and compression, more scene and less narrative, all beautiful and exciting restrictions to my mind."[1]

Taylor's short stories exemplify her technique as a writer. In the short-story genre, her craft is more clearly defined than in the novel. In two articles published in the *Writer,* she explains how two aspects of composition are all important to her: backgrounds and what she calls "illuminating details."

Unlike for writers like Jane Austen and Ivy Compton Burnett whom Taylor greatly admires, backgrounds are an essential part of Taylor's characters. Curious, strange, disturbing places set her mind to work and start a train of creative speculations: "I love places out-of-season, winter seaside resorts with everything shut down, a Greek island settling in for the winter."[2] Her short stories display a great variety of backgrounds. Besides the usual Thames Valley villages, Taylor investigates seaside resorts, country mansions, bed-sitting rooms, an old-fashioned department store, a French country inn, Moroccan resorts. Taylor's range of backgrounds is much wider in her stories than in her novels.

As she often sees herself as a pictorial artist, Taylor confesses that, although no good as a painter, she has tried to draw the backgrounds of her stories. Always precise in her descriptions, yet never naturalistic, Taylor is intent to attract her readers, not to deter them by descriptions of the seediest aspects of life. Her role as a writer remains unobtrusive, however: "When I move characters from place to place, I like to go with them. I am rather like a ghost, unobserved; and *they* are the real ones at that moment."[3]

Taylor's writing methods display great frugality in her selection of chosen details which are to enlighten her readers. Defining details as "strokes of reality, highlights, dashes of colours; breath to the abstract, death to the vague,"[4] Taylor emphasizes their vital role in the construction of a story. Her writing revolves around such meaningful details which, taken individually, can herald a whole story: seeing a blind man on a bus, noticing a waiter on his day off, watching a West Indian running in the rain. "A glimpse can be enough," Taylor notes. "I could never tell how I came to begin to write a novel. It is a complicated business. But, with every short story I have written, I can look back and say, with certainty, '*Thus* it began.' "[5]

Taylor subscribes to Isherwood's description of literary receptiveness: "I am a camera with its shutter open, quite passive, recording not thinking. Recording the man shaving at the window opposite and the woman in the kimono washing her hair. Some day, all this will have to be developed, carefully fixed, printed."[6]

Besides her discreet yet vital reliance upon details, what makes Taylor's stories so fascinating to read may well be her crystallization of one particular "moment of being." Taylor writes that, in short stories, "There may be something therein that may attain perfection, as novels never do, some magic distillation, almost certainly an intensity of experience."[7] She manages to capture brief moments of awareness, loaded with significance. Sudden revelations, first contacts with life or death, paroxysms of boredom, bliss, or regrets—her characters, she implies, will never be the same again. Yet the turmoil of emotions which they often experience in Taylor's stories are mostly described quietly. Even though Taylor stresses "immediate impact" and "suggestiveness" as the desirable attributes for her stories, she can be neither forceful nor vibrant. As in her novels, her restraint remains her principal attribute in the short-story genre.

Taylor's scope and range, in the short-story genre, is far broader than in her novels. Above all, she studies wider social strata than the limited social field to which she confines her novels. While they deal almost exclusively with the upper-middle-class residents of the Thames Valley or of elegant London suburbs, her short stories show a much less selective attitude. Taylor feels more comfortable in handling the lower classes in her stories. Minorities also become a part of her world; several short stories describe the lives of young West Indians. Taylor's stories are also filled with sales ladies, publicans' wives, charwomen, lonely spinsters, famous writers, governesses, factory workers, old women, blind men. The breadth that Taylor offers may remind the reader of a cross-section of village life, from the highest to the lowest: "Village life with its wider differences—in every social sense—seems a better background for a woman novelist, and certainly more congenial to me."[8] Taylor presents her readers with the "slice of life" which so much fascinates her.

Few short stories deal with the privileged few who abound in her novels. In fact, Taylor uses her short stories as a vehicle to express social discomfort and unease. A reviewer once made the interesting wish that "Miss Taylor would stop insisting so on her equation of social maladroitness with moral and intellectual superiority."[9] The statement refers to a recurring pattern in Taylor's stories: she almost invariably presents socially inept characters with considerable sympathy. Her stories also reveal perceptibly more class-consciousness than her novels and are, consequently, more indicative of the time in which she lives and writes.

Taylor's short stories fall into three categories. The majority of them consists of small psychological dramas, short-lived—but intense—experiences that leave the characters thoroughly shaken. A blind man contrives to be taken to the fair by a bunch of cronies who desert him once there. A newlywed couple, in a hotel room, become the unwilling witnesses to a deadly marital fight next door, which frees their own latent hostility toward each other. In each volume of short stories, Taylor also includes a few stories that are pure social comedy. A happy gregarious man on his wedding night has a few drinks in the bar and forgets all about his anxious new bride waiting for him in their hotel room. A gauche young girl at an important social function commits a social faux pas by telling the same story twice to the same man. Finally, in each volume, Taylor inserts one or two anecdotes. These stories differ from the rest mostly through Taylor's obvious intention to describe an isolated incident out of context. The social background is nonexistent or blurred and the characters are sketchily drawn. "Fly Paper" describes the misadventure happening to one not-so-smart young girl who, having been importuned by a man on a bus, gets rescued by a strange woman who later turns out to be the man's accomplice. "Swan Moving" describes the drastic changes brought to a village and its inhabitants by the magical appearance of a swan on its pond's surface.

Hester Lilly and Twelve Short Stories

Taylor's short stories differ greatly in length. "Hester Lilly," which gives its name to the volume, is closer to a novel whereas some of the other stories are mere sketches.

"Hester Lilly" is a poignant tale about the decay of love. A young girl comes to live in a school with her cousin Robert, the headmaster, and his wife Muriel. Young Hester's feelings of loss and loneliness, for she has lost both parents, soon turn to love for her elderly cousin, but Muriel had been expecting this development. "Hester Lilly" shows how scheming and plotting, by killing mutual esteem, can slowly destroy a marriage. Feeling threatened by the young girl, Muriel does her utmost to keep her at bay, first by minimizing her feelings for Robert, then by attempting to push her into someone else's arms. Her husband, who feels selfless love for Hester—a dangerous feeling, for it damages his marriage to a selfish woman without bringing in any feeling of guilt—sees her maneuvers with increasing repulsion. The bewildered young girl, who does not know that she is being manipulated, flees into a hasty marriage to a young man she barely knows. Ironically, Muriel wins the fight, but it has cost her the very thing she wanted to keep: her husband's love: "If I can never love her again, he thought, why is it Hester's fault? It is she, Muriel, who destroyed it, let it slip from her, and then, in trying to have it back again, broke it forever."[10]

Muriel's symbolical dream, at the end of the story, epitomizes her dubious interference in Hester's life. The "sacrificial cake" which she sees herself making for Hester's wedding symbolizes the immolation of the young girl onto the older woman's altar. Muriel, who worked at saving her own marriage, never saw that the destruction was engineered by her own calculations and therefore came from within.

Another story, entitled "Shadows of Love," presents an equally dispirited picture of married life. It describes one dejected evening in the life of an embittered woman, Ida, who cannot come to terms with her life as a wife and mother. In front of a friend, she belittles her own existence. Taylor creates a situation comedy by emphasizing her friend's anxiety to be offered a drink whereas frustration overwhelms his hostess: " 'I have nothing,' she said moodily and dramatically. He looked surprised and alarmed. 'The empty days,' she continued, to his great relief, 'the long, empty days' " (194).

"I Live in a World of Make Believe" is perhaps one of Taylor's best short stories. The very amusing tale relates the countless efforts through which a disgruntled housewife puts herself in order to impress the aristocratic neighbor whom she has invited to tea. Taylor's irony is given full play when, instead of the expected Lady Luna, the socially undesirable Auntie Flo shows up for tea. Finally, when it appears that the bitter hostess's efforts have been wasted, a telephone call announces her that her careless neighbor will visit her the next day instead.

In one of her stories, "A Red-Letter Day," Taylor uses the interesting device of borrowing her characters from one of her novels, *A View of the Harbour.* The story describes the very trying day that Tory Foyle spends while visiting her son Edward at school. The perceptible relief which both mother and son experience when the day comes to an end also underlines the inadequacy that Tory constantly feels as a mother.

Taylor's stories sometimes have a symbolical significance. The anecdotal "Swan Moving" is an interesting piece of fiction about the radical changes that one small incident can bring in the lives of many. The arrival of a swan on a village pond causes the villagers to wake up and shake off their indifference. Strangers come to see the new diversion; the whole village becomes restless as the concept of charm slowly infiltrates itself. When the water level in the pond gets low, the villagers, led by their vicar, set themselves the delicate task of moving the swan to another more distant pond, after which they go home contentedly: "Their lives had been touched so lightly by magic that perhaps only the seeds of a legend were left, or less—no trace at all—but they felt easeful, thinking of the swan in his new home" (210). Ironically, in the last scene of the story, the swan, its mission done, takes off again forever.

It has been argued that Taylor's characters "lay bare vulgar indecencies, revealing human beings at their worst: arid, lustful, frustrated and futile."[11] *Hester Lilly,* which presents a rather glum vision of man, may be the least optimistic of Taylor's collections of short stories. Despite a dejected form of humor, the volume conveys a general impression of uneasiness, disillusionment, and frustration and, as such, cannot truly be seen as most representative of Taylor's talent as a short-story writer.

The Blush and Other Stories

The stories which make up Taylor's second volume bear her trademark more clearly than the earlier ones did. Some of the fascinating little tales could have been developed into novels. It is also true to note, however, that the stories do not appear salvaged from the wreck of a novel. There is a wealth of material present, but sufficient concision and unity to round them into short stories. "A Troubled State of Mind," in particular, has enough complexity for a novel. The story describes the difficult situation in which an eighteen-year-old girl finds herself when, coming back from a year spent in a Swiss school, she finds that her best friend has become her stepmother. Taylor excels at describing the slow but inexorable deterioration of the relationship between the two girls, as well as the deep despondency and envy which soon becomes the fate of the young wife.

The Blush is a less dispirited collection of short stories than *Hester Lilly.* The stories deal mostly with the constant isolation in which human beings find themselves—one of Taylor's recurring themes. In the case of "The Letter-Writers," Taylor deals more particularly with the refusal to face life, to go through what may be a shattering experience. The fairly pathetic story studies the various ways in which people misrepresent each other. A famous author and an obscure woman have exchanged letters for years. When they finally meet, an experience which threatens their well-protected relationship, they suddenly feel that the tenuous yet enduring connection between them might snap. In a final revelation, the woman becomes aware that she has fallen in love with her pen-friend, yet she immediately struggles to hide this too real fact and to rebuild their peaceful and safe letter-writing relationship as if nothing had happened.

The Blush also includes some of the finest examples of Taylor's social comedy. The story that gives its name to the book describes the complex relationship between a childless woman and her prolific, garrulous charwoman whose life, largely spent in beer-drinking, fascinates her prim and proper employer. When the charwoman becomes pregnant again, her husband comes to beg the austere employer to ease up on the cocktail parties and other night events to give his wife a rest. When the meaning of his intervention finally dawns on Mrs. Allen, she starts blushing, hence the name of the story: "She was glad that she was alone, for she could feel her face, her throat, even the tops of her arms burning, and she went over to a looking-glass and studied with great interest this strange phenomenon."[12]

In another story, "Summer Schools," Taylor combines, with great success, comedy and fine psychological dilemma, and her two characters also have tragic dimensions. Ursula plans to visit a newly married friend during her summer vacation. Her sister Melanie, who resents those plans, decides to enroll, out of spite, in a summer school. Taylor shows the ironic disparity between the accounts that both women give of their time. While Ursula, who has had an exciting time, tries to belittle her vacation, Melanie, who has suffered great boredom, tries to make much of hers.

According to a critic, *The Blush* describes situations "that are intrinsically absurd except to the characters involved."[13] Taylor, who has a talent for dealing with absurdity, manages to display both its amusing and its pathetic facets. The utmost example of absurdity may reside in the anecdotal "The True Primitive." Mr. Ransome is a "self-educated lock-keeper who not only turns out oil-paintings but bawls about Dostoievski and Nietzsche in the family circle."[14] The climax occurs when simple, straightforward Lily, who wants to go out with one of Ransome's sons, gets a glimpse of him sitting naked in his parlor: "Through the narrow slit between the shutters she had not seen the two sons, sitting unwillingly but dutifully behind their easels. Terror, in any case, had quite put the thought of Harry out of her mind. She was afraid that Mr. Ransome would come leaping out of the house after her and chase her down the towing path, naked and mad as he was, shouting Balzac and Voltaire after her" (93–94). As Kingsley Amis points out, Taylor's ferocious vein displays best her ability to handle absurdity.

A Dedicated Man and Other Stories

A Dedicated Man contains more distinctive stories of the same vein as *The Blush*. The third collection of short stories is also very English in style, maybe more so than the two previous volumes. A reviewer notes: "The present collection proves anew that English life, with its labyrinthine intricacies of rank and relationships, lends itself as readily as ever to presenting human upheavals in the barely perceptible tilt of an eyebrow or a quarter-tone rise in voice. It reveals also Miss Taylor's ability to create clearly defined little worlds of convincing characters and to set them in motion, quietly moving them into positions where they will reveal themselves."[15]

Once again, Taylor's frugality and restraint are displayed to the best of her advantage. Her twelve stories are mostly psychological dramas, ending with a twist: a sudden revelation exposes the whole dilemma as absurd. These "tiny, valuable moments of truth"[16] prove that the social drama which has been enacted in vain is consequently ludicrous. In Taylor's third collection of short stories even the social comedy fails to amuse and constantly strikes a note of slight discomfort. The title story describes a dedicated waiter, Wilcox, who keeps up the pretense of being married to a waitress, Edith, so as to keep his job in a good hotel. The deception goes on for years until his "wife" starts taking her role a little too seriously, in particular regarding the fate of their fictional son. Her subsequent disappearance puts an ambiguous end to Wilcox's role-playing but the final twist in the story resides in the discovery by irreproachable Wilcox of stolen silverware in his alleged wife's drawers.

In "Girl Reading," Taylor draws a parallel between what may appear as two irreconciliable worlds. A young girl from a poor background comes to stay with her wealthy school-friend's family. Besides money, the Lippmanns have a lot to offer which young Etta has never known before: warmth, fantasy, and romance. When her mother comes to fetch her, Etta suffers much anguish and self-consciousness. Taylor's talent consists in drawing out, with great delicacy, her characters' conflicting feelings in the tricky situation: "Seeing the lawns, the light reflected from the water, later this large, bright room, and the beautiful poppy-seed cake the Hungarian cook had made for tea, she understood completely and felt pained. She could see then, with Etta's eyes, their own dark, narrow house, and she thought of the lonely hours she spent there reading on days of imprisoning rain."[17] The happy ending—an unusual feature—shows Etta suddenly becoming aware that, through love, she belongs in the Lippmanns' world.

In "The Thames Spread Out," Taylor explores her concern with wasted lives. It is a sad and dispirited story about a woman who lives alone in her small house by the river, waiting for Friday nights and her lover to stop by and see her. When the Thames suddenly overflows, the crisis brought about makes Rose suddenly aware of the aimlessness of her life. When the water subsides, she too decides to make changes in her life; she packs her suitcase and walks out of her house for ever.

In *A Dedicated Man*, the prevailing mood is slightly different from Taylor's previous volumes. Most of the stories display an astringent form of wit, showing Taylor as not immediately as entertaining as in *The Blush*, for example, but in perfect command of her writing and of the genre.

The Devastating Boys and Other Stories

Published in 1972, *The Devastating Boys* may be Taylor's best volume of short stories. As in *A Dedicated Man*, the stories are sharply individualized. Called by a reviewer "a pastel stylist, a celebrant of delicately-drawn losers,"[18] Taylor presents characters who have also been described as "English lightweight, well-meaning, silly, harmless."[19] They include an Oxford professor's timid wife, a sour widow chaperoning an unstable young girl, a lonely West Indian, a nosy schoolgirl, a newlywed couple, and two school mistresses. Taylor's wide assortment of characters share a sense isolation or, as it has been noted, "Each character is in search of a feeling that is not there, spiritually, psychologically, geographically."[20] In "Tall Boy," a young West Indian who lives in complete solitude in a bed-sitting-room in London, tries to find a way of making his lonely birthday a memorable occasion, first by sending himself a card, then by wearing his best suit to work. The simple story is infused with a mixture of humor and compassion that reveals Taylor at her very best.

In her last collection of short stories, Taylor also toys with absurdity. In "The Excursion to the Source," young Polly falls off a cliff to her death, because she cannot see very well and mistakes a piece of blue paper for a gentian. In "Flesh," a lonely widower on a vacation abroad checks into a hotel with the cheerful publican's wife whom he has just met, only to be waylaid by a sudden attack of gout. In "In and Out the Houses," an interfering schoolgirl manages to create complete turmoil in her village simply by spreading about the bits of information that she has gathered in her constant visiting. Taylor's way of dealing with absurdity is wholly successful, for she presents her preposterous situations with both convincing seriousness and cool, amused detachment.

In her four collections of short stories, Taylor breaks no new ground. She nevertheless broadens her scope and displays her perfected technique in a clearer, less ambiguous manner than in her twelve novels.

Chapter Nine
Conclusion

Richard Austen once described Taylor's novels as "sad, sardonic, compassionate; full of a sense of loneliness and betrayal, of a society which has lost its roots in the past and cannot comprehend the tragic ironies of the present."[1] It seems inaccurate, however, to classify her novels as "period pieces." Taylor goes beyond giving a sociological account of her time. If, as Richard Austen notes, her novels are permeated with the ambiance of the postwar world, the social connotations seem incidental to her deeper concerns. While social pressures and social distinctions are used to reinforce her plots, they do not constitute the essence of her work. Taylor's recurring themes are mostly loneliness, isolation, failure to relate to one another, wasted lives—as many dispiriting notions which pervade her fiction. Taylor portrays human beings as constantly failing each other and implies that this is the source of all hardships. Yet, in spite of this grim view of human relationships, Taylor also infuses her novels with the existentialist belief in man's intrinsic worth. In spite of all the ordeals which shake her character's lives, Taylor indicates that they have the ability to survive. In her fictional world, only a few are marked as victims: Vesey Macmillan, Dermot Heron, Martha Larkin. Taylor justifies their inability to cope with life by a fundamental weakness in their makeup. Most of her characters are strong individuals who share a basic self-reliance and fundamental strength.

In a world without God, Taylor resorts to a fine, and often highly developed, moral sense to provide guidelines in her fiction. In spite of her totally unobtrusive role as the narrator, Taylor conveys subtle but unequivocal disapproval when her characters infringe upon her own moral rules. Her moral sense promotes dignity, independence, and honesty, but, most of all, solidarity between human beings. Not unlike that of existentialists, Taylor's work carries the strong implication that whereas individuals have a duty toward themselves they have an equally important duty toward each other.

Despite her basic belief in man, however, Taylor's fiction is often pervaded by a form of latent pessimism. Although none of her novels or short stories is permeated with either violence or ferocity or the presence of evil forces—unlike that of Murdoch or Spark—Taylor often hints at dark undercurrents that, somehow, never crystallize. *A Wreath of Roses* is the only novel in which evil materializes under the shape of one character, Richard Elton. Taylor's quiet world is never shattered by violence. What she denounces as negative forces are the mediocrity of her characters, the quiet egotism that individuals cultivate in their daily lives, their petty deceptions and various self-delusions. Kingsley Amis writes: "Mrs. Taylor's concern is often with the contrast between the public and the private face, both as they are and as their owners take them to be, and her diffident pity is reserved for those who, misunderstanding their isolation, cannot recognize help and drive it away."[2] In Taylor's world, self-deception prevails and the weak go to the wall. It is a pessimistic world, but Taylor's gentleness and resignation take the edge of it away.

Taylor's sad insights into grim truths do not make her novels gloomy, nevertheless. An accomplished writer, Taylor manages to achieve balance in her novels by tempering her often dejected comments with the warmth of her social comedy. Taylor also attributes a basic sense of humor to her characters. Difficulties and hardships do not overwhelm them because, in the midst of chaos, they pause to reflect: "I can't help seeing the funny side of it." The recurring phrase expresses Taylor's belief in the basic survival instinct of her characters. Whereas Amis's heroes are tragic despite the constantly high comedy level of his novels, Taylor's heroes are not tragic despite the tragic situations in which they find themselves. Through one of her characters, Taylor expresses her belief that there is need for a form of positive thinking to overcome life's senselessness. One of Taylor's characters, who calls herself an optimist, knows exactly "how deeply pessimistic one must be in the first place to need the sort of optimism she now had at her command."[3]

Taylor's work leaves an impression of deep quietness, re-

straint, and sobriety. Without forceful denunciations, but also
without vibrancy, Taylor delivers her well-bred, quiet message.
And this may be where she errs. In a literary world where
anger, violence, and ferocity are keywords, Taylor's dispassionate tone may well do her a great disservice.

Some critics—Walter Allen is one of them—find her novels
unemphatic and short on substance. They recognize—and perhaps distrust—her perfect mastery of the English language, the
smooth elegance of her prose, the simple precision of her style.
Yet when they attempt to find a universal significance, they
fail to transcend the simple stories: "Miss Taylor must be one
of my blind spots. I recognize her virtues. She writes very well
indeed and her sensibility goes hand in hand with a nicely astringent wit. . . . Technically, her stories can hardly be faulted.
But what do they amount to?"[4]

Critics have difficulty accepting Elizabeth Taylor for what she
is. Her perfect mastery of the language may well make her
appear more ambitious than she really is. She, in fact, writes
domestic novels in the tradition of Jane Austen and she implicitly
accepts the limitations of the genre. As Robert Liddell notes,
"limited" is not necessarily a derogatory comment about any
writer.[5] Taylor writes within a certain tradition, about a certain
class of people whom she knows well, about places where she
has lived all her life. Her vision of the world, which she conveys
in her fiction, is that of Frances, the artist in *A Wreath of Roses:*
"Trying to check life itself, she thought, to make some of the
hurrying everyday things immortal, to paint the everyday things
with tenderness and intimacy—the dirty café, with its pock-
marked mirrors as if they had been shot at, its curly hat-stands,
its stained marble under the yellow light; wet pavements; an
old woman yawning. With tenderness and intimacy."[6] Taylor
concentrates on the most simple, the most humble, the most
familiar aspects of life. Her talent prevents her from ever becoming trivial. What appeals to the many who enjoy her novels is
the delicacy and good taste that pervade her writing.

The most remarkable feature about Taylor's novels and short
stories may be the discreet—yet efficient—way in which she
conveys pathos. Steering clear of easy sentimentality, Taylor
works her way through implications and understatements. Her

reliance on the significant detail, the revealing gesture, the moment of revelation—devices amounting to literary impressionism—give a particularly rich, colorful texture to the narrative of her novels and short stories.

Granville Hicks once expressed the opinion that "Like Jane Austen and like Henry James, whom she also admires, she sacrifices breadth for depth and gets the best of the bargain."[7] Taylor's novels, "moving through a restricted cycle of emotional keys," dealing with a limited social field, allow her to display the qualities that have won her well-deserved critical acclaim and should ensure her a lasting reputation as one of England's most perceptive novelists: her deep understanding of human foibles and her profoundly healthy sense of humor.

Notes and References

Chapter One

1. Kenneth Allsop, *The Angry Decade* (London: Peter Owen, 1958), 13.
2. Sam Hynes, "The 'Poor Sod' as Hero," *Commonweal* 64, no. 2 (13 April 1956):51.
3. Allsop, *The Angry Decade,* 17.
4. Frank Hilton, "Britain's New Class," *Encounter* 10, no. 2 (February 1958):59.
5. See Malcolm Bradbury's introduction to *A Passage to India: A Casebook* (London: Macmillan, 1970), 15.
6. Leslie A. Fiedler, "The Un-Angry Young Men," *Encounter* 10, no. 1 (January 1958):9.
7. See Frances J. Wallace, "Elizabeth Taylor," *Wilson Library Bulletin* 22 (April 1948):580.
8. See Stanley J. Kunitz and Howard Haycraft, eds., *Twentieth Century Authors,* supp. 1 (New York: H. W. Wilson Co., 1955), 985.
9. Wallace, "Elizabeth Taylor," 580.
10. *A View of the Harbour* (New York, 1947), 66–67.
11. Kunitz and Haycraft, eds., *Twentieth Century Authors,* 985.
12. Quoted by Wallace, "Elizabeth Taylor," 580.
13. Kunitz and Haycraft, eds., *Twentieth Century Authors,* 985.
14. William Cooper, *Scenes from Life* (New York: Charles Scribner's Sons, 1961), 260.
15. "Setting a Scene," *Writer* 78, no. 7 (July 1965):9.
16. *A Wreath of Roses* (New York, 1949), 42.
17. Kingsley Amis, "At Mrs Taylor's," *Spectator* 109 (14 June 1957):784.
18. Quoted on the dust jacket of *A Game of Hide and Seek* (New York, 1951).
19. Anthony Burgess, *The Novel Now* (London: Faber & Faber, 1969), 123.
20. David Lodge, *The Novelist at the Crossroads* (Ithaca: Cornell University Press, 1971), 18.
21. Kingsley Amis, "Laughter's To Be Taken Seriously," *New York Times Book Review,* 7 July 1957, 1.
22. L. P. Hartley, "The Literary Lounger," *Sketch* 203 (October 1945):218.

23. Elizabeth Bowen, *"Palladian,"* Tatler, 25 February 1946, 23.

24. Rosamond Lehmann, *"Palladian,"* Listener, 10 March 1946, 17.

25. Brigid Brophy, "Elizabeth Taylor," in *Don't Never Forget: Collected Views and Reviews* (London: Jonathan Cape, 1966), 163.

26. Amis, "At Mrs Taylor's," 786.

27. Arthur Mizener, "In the Austen Vein," *New Republic* 129 (2 November 1953):25.

28. Gerald Sykes, "In Matters of Love," *New York Times Book Review,* 26 September 1954, 5.

Chapter Two

1. Henry Rago, *"Palladian,"* Commonweal 45 (21 March 1947):569.

2. See William Cooper, *Scenes from Provincial Life* (London: Jonathan Cape, 1950), John Wain, *Hurry on Down* (London: Secker & Warburg, 1953), Kingsley Amis, *Lucky Jim* (London: Victor Gollancz, 1953), and John Braine, *Room at the Top* (London: Eyre & Spottiswoode, 1957).

3. *At Mrs Lippincote's* (London, 1945), 26; hereafter cited in the text.

4. Virginia Woolf, *To the Lighthouse* (London: Everyman's, 1964), 40.

5. *Palladian* (New York, 1946), 42; hereafter cited in the text.

6. Helen Woodward, "Wherein a Shy and Delicate Heroine Follows the Footsteps of Jane Eyre," *Chicago Sun Book Week,* 23 February 1947, 10.

7. Rayner Heppenstall, "New Novels: *Palladian,"* New Statesman and Nation 32 (9 November 1946):343.

8. J. W. Chase, "Fresh Talent, Sensitive Spirit," *New York Herald Tribune Weekly Book Review,* 16 February 1947, 3.

Chapter Three

1. "Briefly Noted: *A View of the Harbour,"* New Yorker, 25 October 1947, 117.

2. Iris Barry, "A Charming Miniature," *New York Herald Tribune Weekly Book Review,* 4 January 1948, 4.

3. *A View of the Harbour* (New York: 1947), 336; hereafter cited in the text.

4. Barry, "A Charming Miniature," 4.

5. H. I'A. Fausset, *"A View of the Harbour,"* Manchester Guardian, 5 September 1947, 3.

6. Quoted by Robert Liddell, "Elizabeth Taylor," in *Contemporary Novelists,* ed. James Vinson (New York, 1972), 1223.

7. *A Wreath of Roses* (New York, 1949), 163; hereafter cited in the text.

8. Woolf, *To the Lighthouse,* 186.

9. Ibid.

10. Donald Barr, "Texture of Experience," *New York Times Book Review,* 13 March 1949, 4.

11. Woolf, *To the Lighthouse,* 186.

12. Ibid.

Chapter Four

1. Amis, "At Mrs Taylor's," 784.

2. Kingsley Amis, "A Gay Scalpel," *Spectator,* 21 November 1959, 708.

3. *Angel* (New York, 1957), 49; hereafter cited in the text.

4. Amis, "A Gay Scalpel," 708.

5. Amis, "At Mrs Taylor's," 786.

6. Ibid.

7. Walter Allen, "New Novels: *The Sleeping Beauty,*" *New Statesman and Nation* 45 (4 April 1953):405.

8. *The Sleeping Beauty* (New York, 1957), 250; hereafter cited in the text.

9. "Human Incongruity," *Times Literary Supplement,* 3 April 1953, 217.

Chapter Five

1. *A Game of Hide and Seek* (New York, 1951), 296; hereafter cited in the text.

2. Liddell, "Elizabeth Taylor," 1224.

3. *In a Summer Season* (New York, 1961), 19; hereafter cited in the text.

4. M. C. Chase, "Touches of the Matchless Jane in a New English Novel," *New York Herald Tribune of Lively Arts,* 12 February 1961, 31.

5. Richard Mayne, "Shoot the Moralist," *New Statesman* 61 (28 April 1961):678.

6. Fanny Butcher, "An Engaging Narrative of English Gentle-Folk," *Chicago Sunday Tribune,* 29 January 1961, 3.

Chapter Six

1. *The Soul of Kindness* (New York, 1964), 152; hereafter cited in the text.

2. J. R. Frakes, "A Unique Garden Variety," *Bookweek,* 12 July 1964, 18.

3. Ibid.

4. Ibid.

5. Brigid Brophy, "Mr Waugh's Eschatology," *New Statesman* 68 (25 September 1964), 450.

6. Ibid.

7. *The Wedding Group* (New York, 1968), 144; hereafter cited in the text.

8. Kingsley Amis, *Lucky Jim* (Harmondsworth: Penguin Books, 1960), 60.

9. "Home From Home," *Times Literary Supplement,* 9 May 1968, 473.

10. Ibid.

11. Nora Sayre, "Violence is Primary," *New York Times Book Review,* 31 March 1968, 40.

12. "Home from Home," 473.

13. Ibid.

Chapter Seven

1. *Mrs Palfrey at the Claremont* (New York, 1971), 3; hereafter cited in the text.

2. Kingsley Amis, "How to Behave," *New Statesman* 82 (27 August 1971):275–76.

3. *Blaming* (New York, 1976), 81; hereafter cited in the text.

4. F. E. De Usabel, *"Blaming," Library Journal* 101 (15 November 1976):2395.

5. Paul Bailey, "Brave Face," *New Statesman* 92 (17 September 1976):380.

6. Rosemary Dinnage, "The Tick of Blood in the Wrist," *Times Literary Supplement,* 10 September 1976, 1096.

Chapter Eight

1. "Some Notes on Writing Stories," *London Magazine* 9, no. 12 (March 1970):9.

2. "Setting a Scene," *Writer* 78, no. 7 (July 1965):10.

3. Ibid.

4. "Choosing Details That Count," *Writer* 83, no. 1 (January 1970):15.

5. "England," *Kenyon Review* 31, no. 4 (1969):471.

6. Quoted by Taylor in "Choosing Details That Count," 44.

7. "Some Notes on Writing Stories," 10.

8. Quoted in Kunitz and Haycraft, eds., *Twentieth Century Authors,* 985.

9. Janet Winn, "A Defense of Shyness," *New Republic* 140 (1 June 1959):21.

10. *Hester Lilly and Twelve Short Stories* (New York, 1954), 62; hereafter cited in the text.

11. R. W. Henderson, "Hester Lilly and Twelve Short Stories," *Library Journal* 79 (1 September 1954):1505.

12. *The Blush and Other Stories* (New York, 1959), 35.

13. "The Characters are English," *Christian Science Monitor,* 9 July 1959, 7.

14. Amis, "A Gay Scalpel," 708.

15. Chad Walsh, "Quiet Life," *Book Week,* 25 July 1965, 14.

16. "Enervating Albatrosses," *Times Literary Supplement,* 1 July 1965, 553.

17. *A Dedicated Man and Other Stories* (New York, 1965), 27; hereafter cited in the text.

18. Martin Levin, *"The Devastating Boys,"* *New York Times Book Review,* 23 April 1972, 41.

19. J. C. Oates, " 'Real' People or Characters," *Book World,* 30 April 1972, 6.

20. Jean Spang, *"The Devastating Boys,"* *Library Journal* 97 (1 April 1972):1349.

Chapter Nine

1. Richard Austen, "The Novels of Elizabeth Taylor," *Commonweal* 62, no. 10 (10 June 1955):258.

2. Amis, "At Mrs Taylor's," 785–86.

3. *Mrs Palfrey at the Claremont,* 85.

4. Walter Allen, "New Short Stories: *The Blush,"* *New Statesman* 56 (20 December 1958):889.

5. See Robert Liddell, "The Novels of Elizabeth Taylor," *Review of English Literature* 1 (April 1960):61.

6. *A Wreath of Roses* (New York, 1949), 41–42; hereafter cited in the text.

7. Granville Hicks, "Amour on the Thames," *Saturday Review* 44 (21 January 1961):62.

Selected Bibliography

PRIMARY SOURCES

1. Novels

A Game of Hide and Seek. London: Peter Davies, 1951; New York: Alfred A. Knopf, 1951.

A View of the Harbour. London: Peter Davies, 1947; New York: Alfred A. Knopf, 1947.

A Wreath of Roses. London: Peter Davies, 1949; New York: Alfred A. Knopf, 1949.

Angel. London: Peter Davies, 1957; New York: Viking Press, 1957.

At Mrs Lippincote's. London: Peter Davies, 1945; New York: Alfred A. Knopf, 1946.

Blaming. London: Chatto & Windus, 1976; New York: Viking Press, 1976.

In a Summer Season. London: Peter Davies, 1961; New York: Viking Press, 1961.

Mrs Palfrey at the Claremont. London: Chatto & Windus, 1971; New York: Viking Press, 1971.

Palladian. London: Peter Davies, 1946; New York, Alfred A. Knopf, 1947.

The Sleeping Beauty. London: Peter Davies, 1953; New York: Viking Press, 1953.

The Soul of Kindness. London: Chatto & Windus, 1964; New York: Viking Press, 1964.

The Wedding Group. London: Chatto & Windus, 1968; New York: Viking Press, 1968.

2. Short Stories

A Dedicated Man and Other Stories. London: Chatto & Windus, 1972; New York: Viking Press, 1972.

Hester Lilly and Twelve Short Stories, London: Peter Davies, 1954; New York: Viking Press, 1954.

The Blush and Other Stories. London: Peter Davies, 1958; New York: Viking Press, 1959.

The Devastating Boys and Other Stories. London: Chatto & Windus, 1972; New York: Viking Press, 1972.

3. Articles
"Choosing Details That Count." *Writer* 83, no. 1 (January 1970):15–
    16.
"England." *Kenyon Review* 31, no. 4 (1969):469–73.
"Some Notes on Writing Stories." *London Magazine* 9, no. 12 (March
    1970):8–10.
"Setting a Scene." *Writer* 78, no. 7 (July 1965):9–10.

SECONDARY SOURCES

Amis, Kingsley. "At Mrs Taylor's." *Spectator,* 14 June 1957, 784,
    786. A brief discussion of Taylor's lack of critical recognition
    and a perceptive study of the comic aspect of *Angel,* seen as "some-
    thing of a new departure."
————. "How to Behave." *New Statesman* 82 (27 August 1971):275–
    76. A review of *Mrs Palfrey at the Claremont* in which Amis com-
    pares Taylor's manner ("funny and appalling lie side by side")
    with Waugh's.
Austen, Richard. "The Novels of Elizabeth Taylor." *Commonweal*
    62, no. 10 (10 June 1955):258–59. Austen discusses Taylor's
    first six novels and points out the recurring themes as well as
    the significant features of her technique.
Bailey, Paul. "Brave Face." *New Statesman* 92 (17 September
    1976):380. Taylor's heroine, Amy Henderson, is seen as one
    of the "brave faces" from her fictional world. A discussion of
    Blaming's "Englishness" and sensitivity.
Brickner, Richard. "Killing with Kindness." *New Republic* 151 (22
    August 1964):30, 32. A discussion of the significant quietness
    that prevails in *The Soul of Kindness,* and of the various examples
    of destructive "kindness" that the novel reveals.
Brown, Catherine Meredith. "Ruffled English Retreat." *Saturday
    Review of Literature* 32 (26 March 1949):12. Sees Taylor's Woolf-
    like ability to capture the essence of the moment in *A Wreath
    of Roses.* A perceptive review that highlights the novel's best fea-
    tures.
Chase, J. W. "Fresh Talent, Sensitive Spirit." *New York Herald Tribune
    Weekly Book Review,* 16 February 1947, 3. *Palladian*'s weaknesses
    are pointed out—characters who are "ghosts of real flesh and
    blood," narrative that lacks purpose—but Taylor's qualities
    are also praised: "fresh talent, a keen ear, sensitive spirit."
    A positive outlook on Taylor's second—and least successful—
    novel.

Dinnage, Rosemary. "The Tick of Blood in the Wrist." *Times Literary Supplement,* 10 September 1976, 1096. Studies *Blaming* as Taylor's last utterance. Sees it as a "gentle close" to her writing career, as less powerful than her earlier novels.

Groberg, Nancy. "Strange, Amazing People." *Saturday Review of Literature* 29 (20 April 1946):15. An American reviewer's reactions to the "Englishness" of *At Mrs Lippincote's.* Confesses that if the characters are very real, "the world is strange." May justify the Americans' reticence toward Taylor's first novel.

Hicks, Granville. "Amour on the Thames." *Saturday Review* 44 (21 January 1961):62. Perceptive comments on Taylor's writing as a whole, and on *In a Summer Season* in particular. Points out that Jane Austen is the only one to whom Taylor can be justly compared.

Janeway, Elizabeth. "How Things Work Out." *New York Times Book Review,* 22 January 1961, 5. Stresses the lack of sense of right and wrong in *In a Summer Season* and the various conflicts within the novel.

————. "Love is a Sad Game." *New York Times Book Review,* 4 March 1951, 5. Praises Taylor's perfection of prose and her clarity of vision. Questions the purpose of *A Game of Hide and Seek,* especially its ambiguous ending.

Liddell, Robert. "Elizabeth Taylor." In *Contemporary Novelists,* edited by James Vinson, 1223–25. New York: St. Martin's Press, 1972. Sees the relative lack of critical appreciation for Taylor's novels as arising from the fact that critics find her world devoid of the "filth and violence" that are marked features of the novel today.

————. "The Novels of Elizabeth Taylor." *A Review of English Literature* 1 (April 1960):54–61. A discussion of the most striking features of Taylor's individuality: in particular, the reality of her pictorial world.

McKitrick, Eric L. "Chronic Cankers." *Saturday Review of Literature* 30 (8 November 1947):18. A positive review of *A View of the Harbour* seen as a tour de force, "one of the most brilliant views of any harbour." The novel's concision, polish, and brilliance are praised.

Mizener, Arthur. "In the Austen Vein." *New Republic* 129 (2 November 1953):25. The article in which Mizener first called Taylor "the modern man's Jane Austen." Sees *The Sleeping Beauty* as an adjustment to the "terrible and comic" conditions of postwar life.

Rosenthal, Lucy. "*Mrs Palfrey at the Claremont.*" *Saturday Review* 54 (31 July 1971):25–26. Points out the contrast between the fullness of emotions revealed in the novel and the cool detachment which Taylor constantly keeps.

Saxon, Alice. "Novel about a Juvenile Novelist." *Commonweal* 67 (25 October 1957):102–3. An answer to the question of the purpose of *Angel*. Sees Angel as psychologically intriguing, and the novel as interesting on the subject of the creative artist.

Sayre, Nora. "Violence is Primary." *New York Times Book Review,* 31 March 1968, 40. Sees Taylor's fiction as permeated with a violence that is hidden behind the constant self-control that her characters exert.

Wallace, Frances. "Elizabeth Taylor." *Wilson Library Bulletin* 22 (April 1948):580. A biographical sketch.

Index